"Once Saved, Always Saved"

TRUTH
or
DELUSION ?

Now therefore ye are . . . built upon
the foundation of the apostles and prophets,
Jesus Christ himself being
the chief corner stone;
in whom all the building fitly framed
together groweth unto an holy
temple in the Lord."

Ephesians 2:19–22

"That they may adorn the doctrine
of God our Saviour in
all things."

Titus 2:10

"Once Saved, Always Saved"

TRUTH or DELUSION?

By Paul M. Landis

Rod and Staff Publishers, Inc.
P.O. Box 3, 14193 Hwy. 172
Crockett, Kentucky 41413
Telephone: (606) 522-4348

Printed in U.S.A.

ISBN 0-7399-0198-2

Catalog no. 2332

6 7 8 9 10 — 15 14 13 12 11 10 09 08 07 06

Contents

Preface

Many churchmen and church members believe that the Bible teaches that once a person is born again by God's grace and made His child, he can never be lost. He is unconditionally saved forever. They believe that the saints are unconditionally, eternally secure.

The Bible teaches us to "**prove all things; hold fast that which is good" (1 Thessalonians 5:21).** This study is an effort to do just that. It is not an effort to consider each tenet of this doctrine. Instead, we are approaching the Word of God with the question, What does God say about the security of those who have become His children?

The critical matter of concern is whether a person who is living in disobedience to God's commandments is prepared to meet Jesus Christ in peace at His coming. What effect does sin have on the life and security of the Christian? Does sin in the life of the child of God affect his relationship with the heavenly Father? Does the teaching in the Bible that says, "**The soul that sinneth, it shall die,**" apply to the

Christian or just to those who have never been saved?

Let the Word speak. God has chosen to reveal Himself and His will for man through the written Word. When we know what the Word says, we have God's answer. At the end of time, in the presence of His glory, majesty, dominion, sovereignty, and power, all men will stand in silence. Jesus Christ, whom God has ordained to judge the world in righteousness will speak in authority. And what He declares there about every man will determine his eternal destiny. And "**we are sure that the judgment of God is according to truth against them which commit such things**" **(Romans 2:2).** Therefore, let us listen carefully to what God has to say to us in His revelation concerning Himself and the salvation He sent His Son to secure for us.

The purpose of this book is to observe what the Bible says about sin; how God defines *salvation* and *saint*; what God's covenant with man is; who will enter the habitation of God's holiness; and how believing "once saved, always saved" influences the way we relate to all the above. This book has been written to help souls who are seeking truth with an honest heart, who want to know from the Word of God that they are ready to meet God in peace, who want the assurance that they are here and now fulfilling His will and purpose in their lives, and who are determined that by God's grace they will do the will of God when they know what it is.

God is a covenant-making God. He designs the terms of the covenant and then offers the covenant and its benefits to man. Man has the privilege to accept or reject those terms. What happens when he accepts God's specific terms? when he rejects them? Never mind the reasonings of man—what seems reasonable or unreasonable to him. God is governed by that which is in agreement with His holy character.

We want to see first what God says on the subject and then compare what men say with that, instead of seeing first what men say. **"To the law and to the testimony: if they speak not according to this word, it is because there is no light in them" (Isaiah 8:20).** John the apostle expresses agreement and adds another dimension: **"He that saith, I know him, and keepeth not his commandments, is a liar, and the truth is not in him. But whoso keepeth his word, in him verily is the love of God perfected: hereby know we that we are in him" (1 John 2:4, 5).**

Inasmuch as we are taking this approach in our study, no apology should be necessary for quoting many verses from the Word of God. God's Word alone is truth. It is our life, our foundation. Jesus said,

"Whosoever cometh to me, and heareth my sayings . . . is like a man which built an house, and digged deep, and laid the foundation on a rock" (Luke 6:47, 48).

Paul M. Landis

1.

The Beginning

The slogan "once saved, always saved" is used to express the belief that once a person has been born again by the Spirit of God, he *can* never, or *will* never, be lost. Unconditional eternal security is another term used to express this concept. Many variations or companion beliefs are held by individuals and/or entire church groups. For example, some contend that once a person is truly saved, he will never backslide or live in sin and that so doing proves that he was never truly saved.

From the beginning of man's existence, Satan has

been suggesting this lie. He opened his interview with Eve in the Garden of Eden by asking:

> **"Yea, hath God said, Ye shall not eat of every tree of the garden? And the woman said unto the serpent, We may eat of the fruit of the trees of the garden: but of the fruit of the tree which is in the midst of the garden, God hath said, Ye shall not eat of it, neither shall ye touch it, lest ye die."**

Now observe the boldness of the serpent (Satan). He said to the woman:

> **"Ye shall not surely die: for God doth know that in the day ye eat thereof, then your eyes shall be opened, and ye shall be as gods, knowing good and evil."**

Satan knew God had spoken, but he defiantly contradicted and challenged what God had said. (See Genesis 3:1–5.)

Were God's words true? Did Adam die? *Yes, he most certainly did.* He was immediately cut off from God. Adam was a perfect, holy being in fellowship with the holy Lord God, a son of God, made in God's own image. But when he sinned against God, God cut him off. He was entirely helpless to change his fallen state. He was in need of a savior, a mediator between himself and his God, one who could reconcile the offense between them.

The promoters of "once saved, always saved" say that once a person is a son of God, he cannot be "unborn," that he is always a son. Yet Adam was a son who was disowned, cast away from his Creator, God. So also are all who continue in sin today. It is Satan who says, as he did in the Garden of Eden, that if a person sins after he is born again, "[he] **shall *not* surely die.**"

For centuries false prophets troubled Israel by deciding what to do with what God commanded His people. In like manner, since the time of Christ, preachers and churches have been declaring that God does not mean what He says, that His Word needs to be interpreted in the light of human reasoning and human experience and is not to be taken too literally. This teaching—that once a person is saved, he can never again be lost or cut off from God; that God will not damn a soul to hell for sins committed after conversion, even though those sins are not repented of or forsaken—has seared and deadened the conscience of many evangelical churches so that they no longer heed God's message about the deadliness of sin. This teaching has borne its horrible fruit. Many believers who call themselves evangelicals are loaded with divers sins, and their churches have no power to do anything about it.

Satan has succeeded in saturating the pulpits and pews of the churches in the West with this attitude toward sin, and the ills of society are the result. The burden of responsibility lies with the preachers who refuse to believe God and to cry out against the sins of those who profess to be His children. There is a famine for the true Word of God. As Amos prophesied:

> **"Behold, the days come, saith the Lord God, that I will send a famine in the land, not a famine of bread, nor a thirst for water, but of hearing the words of the Lord: and they shall wander from sea to sea, and from the north even to the east, they shall run to and fro to seek the word of the Lord, and shall not find it" (Amos 8:11, 12).**

2.

What Does the Bible Say?

"Sin is the transgression of the law" (1 John 3:4).

"All unrighteousness is sin" (1 John 5:17).

"Therefore to him that knoweth to do good, and doeth it not, to him it is sin" (James 4:17).

"He that doubteth is damned if he eat, because he eateth not of faith: for whatsoever is not of faith is sin" (Romans 14:23).

"The soul that sinneth, it shall die"

(Ezekiel 18:4).

"The righteousness of the righteous shall not deliver him in the day of his transgression: as for the wickedness of the wicked, he shall not fall thereby in the day that he turneth from his wickedness; neither shall the righteous be able to live for his righteousness in the day that he sinneth. . . . When the righteous turneth from his righteousness, and committeth iniquity, he shall even die thereby" (Ezekiel 33:12, 18).

These Bible verses teach that disobedience to God's Word is sin in the life of any person, be he saint or sinner.

Paul wrote to the saints at Rome that God

"will render to every man according to his deeds . . . for there is no respect of persons with God" (Romans 2:6, 11).

This principle is taught consistently in both Testaments, as we shall observe in a later chapter dealing with the testimony of the Book of Hebrews.

The prophet Jeremiah described the false prophets in his day as those who got their message out of their own hearts, not from God.

"Thus saith the Lord of hosts, Hearken not

unto the words of the prophets that prophesy unto you: they make you vain: they speak a vision of their own heart, and not out of the mouth of the Lord. They say still unto them that despise me, The Lord hath said, Ye shall have peace; and they say unto every one that walketh after the imagination of his own heart, No evil shall come upon you. . . . Behold, I am against the prophets, saith the Lord, that use their tongues, and say, He saith" (Jeremiah 23:16, 17, 31).

"But there were false prophets also among the people, even as there shall be false teachers among you, who privily shall bring in damnable heresies, even denying the Lord that bought them, and bring upon themselves swift destruction. And many shall follow their pernicious ways; by reason of whom the way of truth shall be evil spoken of. . . . For when they speak great swelling words of vanity, they allure through the lusts of the flesh, through much wantonness, those that were clean escaped from them who live in error. While they promise them liberty, they themselves are the servants of corruption: for of whom a man is overcome, of the same is he

brought in bondage. For if after they have escaped the pollutions of the world through the knowledge of the Lord and Saviour Jesus Christ, they are again entangled therein, and overcome, the latter end is worse with them than the beginning. For it had been better for them not to have known the way of righteousness, than, after they have known it, to turn from the holy commandment delivered unto them. But it is happened unto them according to the true proverb, The dog is turned to his own vomit again; and the sow that was washed to her wallowing in the mire" (2 Peter 2:1, 2, 18–22).

"**The latter end** [of continuing in or returning to their sins] **is worse with them than the beginning.**" In the beginning they were "**dead in trespasses and sins . . . and were by nature the children of wrath" (Ephesians 2:1, 3).** The Bible says, "**It had been better for them not to have known the way of righteousness,**" than to have known it and then turn from it.

Now let us look at God's view of sin, as the disciple of love explained it.

"**Whosoever abideth in him sinneth not:**

whosoever sinneth hath not seen him, neither known him. Little children, let no man deceive you: he that doeth righteousness is righteous, even as he is righteous. He that committeth sin is of the devil; for the devil sinneth from the beginning" (1 John 3:6–8).

The Greek tense employed here for the word *committeth* conveys the thought of continuing in sin or of repeated action. And in the next verse quoted below, the same Greek tense is used for the first *sin,* but the tense used for the second *sin* implies point action.

"My little children, these things write I unto you, that ye sin not [repeated action]. **And if any man sin** [point action], **we have an advocate with the Father, Jesus Christ the righteous" (1 John 2:1).**

This means that if a Christian is misled by Satan and sins but is then penitent, he has an advocate before the Father, and forgiveness. But if a person is bound in a practice or habit of sin that he will not or cannot put away, there is no forgiveness. Only when he repents in godly sorrow and forsakes sin by faith in the power of Jesus' blood is there forgiveness and cleansing.

The Bible teaches that salvation includes:

1. Forgiveness for past sins (Romans 3:25; Ephesians 1:7);
2. Cleansing from the defilement of sin (1 John 1:7; Revelation 1:5); and
3. Deliverance from sin in all the temptations we face throughout life (Romans 8:37; 1 Corinthians 15:57; 2 Corinthians 2:14).

3.

The Teachings of Jesus

"Blessed are the pure in heart: for they shall see God" (Matthew 5:8).

"Then said Jesus to those Jews which believed on him, If ye continue in my word, then are ye my disciples indeed; and ye shall know the truth, and the truth shall make you free. . . . Verily, verily, I say unto you, Whosoever committeth sin is the servant of sin. . . . If the Son therefore shall make you free, ye shall be free indeed" (John 8:31, 32, 34, 36).

Jesus used light and darkness to illustrate that God and Satan, right and wrong, do not mix. He declares that it is impossible to serve both.

> **"The light of the body is the eye: if therefore thine eye be single, thy whole body shall be full of light. But if thine eye be evil, thy whole body shall be full of darkness. If therefore the light that is in thee be darkness, how great is that darkness! No man can serve two masters: for either he will hate the one, and love the other; or else he will hold to the one, and despise the other. Ye cannot serve God and mammon" (Matthew 6:22–24).**

The whole tenor of the Scriptures is that God has ordained the righteous to be separate from the unrighteous and that the righteous shall assume the responsibility to have it so. In keeping with this, Jesus said:

> **"Enter ye in at the strait gate: for wide is the gate, and broad is the way, that leadeth to destruction, and many there be which go in thereat: because strait is the gate, and narrow is the way, which leadeth unto life, and few there be that find it" (Matthew 7:13, 14).**

From Jesus' own explanation in the verses that

follow, we gather that both those on the broad way and those on the narrow way profess to be God's children. Jesus was speaking of the obedient and the disobedient, the faithful and the unfaithful—all who profess that they believe and serve God. He was clarifying the difference between a saving faith and a faith that will not save the soul. Those who are made free by the truth unto holiness of life are on the narrow way that leads to eternal life, while those who, in spite of their profession, continue in disobedience to the Word of God are on the broad way that leads to destruction.

"Beware of false prophets, which come to you in sheep's clothing, but inwardly they are ravening wolves. Ye shall know them by their fruits. Do men gather grapes of thorns, or figs of thistles? Even so every good tree bringeth forth good fruit; but a corrupt tree bringeth forth evil fruit. A good tree cannot bring forth evil fruit, neither can a corrupt tree bring forth good fruit. Every tree that bringeth not forth good fruit is hewn down, and cast into the fire. Wherefore by their fruits ye shall know them. Not every one that saith unto me, Lord, Lord, shall enter into the kingdom of heaven; but he that doeth the will of my Father which is in

heaven. Many will say to me in that day, Lord, Lord, have we not prophesied in thy name? and in thy name have cast out devils? and in thy name done many wonderful works? And then will I profess unto them, I never knew you: depart from me, ye that work iniquity" (Matthew 7:15–23).

Wolves in sheep's clothing are hypocrites. What shall then be said of those who claim to be sheep, but appear in wolves' clothing? **"Ye shall know them by their fruits."** The outward actions, manner of dress, speech, and activities unmistakably testify of the relationship of the heart to God.

To make His point clear to His hearers, Jesus emphasized that the only way to be His disciple and to remain saved is to obey His Word.

"Therefore whosoever heareth these sayings of mine, and doeth them, I will liken him unto a wise man, which built his house upon a rock: and the rain descended, and the floods came, and the winds blew, and beat upon that house; and it fell not: for it was founded upon a rock. And every one that heareth these sayings of mine, and doeth them not, shall be likened unto a foolish man, which built his

house upon the sand: and the rain descended, and the floods came, and the winds blew, and beat upon that house; and it fell: and great was the fall of it. And . . . the people were astonished at his doctrine: for he taught them as one having authority, and not as the scribes" (Matthew 7:24–29).

Then the cry goes up that such a belief is legalism! Legalism is the belief that we can save ourselves by keeping a certain law or laws. But obedience is the evidence that we believe Him; that we have been cleansed from the defilement of sin; that we have been **"delivered . . . from the power of darkness, and** [have been] **translated . . . into the kingdom of his dear Son" (Colossians 1:13).** However, if we practice sin and justify ourselves in it after we have been born again, we again become sinners. Sin is the factor that separates man from God.

Jesus explained to the multitude who His disciples are when He said:

"If ye continue in my word, then are ye my disciples indeed" (John 8:31).

"And he looked round about on them which sat about him, and said, Behold my mother and my brethren! For whosoever shall

do the will of God, the same is my brother, and my sister, and mother" (Mark 3:34, 35).

Jesus also taught that forgiveness of our sins is dependent upon how we relate to others day by day.

"If ye forgive men their trespasses, your heavenly Father will also forgive you: but if ye forgive not men their trespasses, neither will your Father forgive your trespasses" (Matthew 6:14, 15).

In the parable of the nobleman, Jesus taught us what God will do with His enemies.

"But those mine enemies, which would not that I should reign over them, bring hither, and slay them before me" (Luke 19:27).

Those men and women who serve their lusts and appetites rather than God are His enemies. Their condition is one of idolatry in the heart. They will be cast into outer darkness forever.

"So shall it be in the end of this world. The Son of man shall send forth his angels, and they shall gather out of his kingdom all things that offend, and them which do iniquity; and shall cast them into a furnace of fire: there shall be wailing and gnashing of teeth. Then shall the righteous shine forth as the sun in

the kingdom of their Father. Who hath ears to hear, let him hear" (Matthew 13:40–43).

Jesus taught His disciples that apostates are dull of hearing. When men choose to believe that disobedience to God's Word does not affect their standing with God, they become dull of hearing. They believe that judgment does not apply to them.

4.

What Does Paul Teach?

CHRIST IS NOT "THE MINISTER OF SIN"

The Book of Galatians, written by Paul, teaches the church that to justify sin in our lives after we have been saved makes Christ a sinner.

> **"But if, while we seek to be justified by Christ, we ourselves also are found sinners, is therefore Christ the minister of sin? God forbid. For if I build again the things which I destroyed, I make myself a transgressor. For**

> **I through the law am dead to the law, that I might live unto God. I am crucified with Christ: nevertheless I live; yet not I, but Christ liveth in me: and the life which I now live in the flesh I live by the faith of the Son of God, who loved me, and gave himself for me. I do not frustrate the grace of God: for if righteousness come by the law, then Christ is dead in vain.**
>
> **"O foolish Galatians, who hath bewitched you, that ye should not obey the truth, before whose eyes Jesus Christ hath been evidently set forth, crucified among you? This only would I learn of you, Received ye the Spirit by the works of the law, or by the hearing of faith? Are ye so foolish? having begun in the Spirit, are ye now made perfect by the flesh? . . . Is the law then against the promises of God? God forbid: for if there had been a law given which could have given life, verily righteousness should have been by the law" (Galatians 2:17–3:3, 21).**

In these verses Paul teaches us that "**by the works of the law shall no flesh be justified" (Galatians 2:16)**, and that to sin after we have been justified by the blood of Jesus makes us sinners again. Therefore, to *live in sin* and justify ourselves in it as Christians makes Christ the minister of sin. Unthinkable!

Paul prayed for the saints in Philippi:

> **"That ye may be sincere and without offence till the day of Christ; being filled with the fruits of righteousness, which are by Jesus Christ, unto the glory and praise of God" (Philippians 1:10, 11).**

"The fruits of righteousness [not sin] . . . **are by Jesus Christ"** in our lives as He lives within. Paul stressed that only in Jesus Christ we are made righteous before God. He gave his own testimony:

> **"And be found in him, not having mine own righteousness, which is of the law, but that which is through the faith of Christ, the righteousness which is of God by faith" (Philippians 3:9).**

Paul then warned the Philippians (and us) that some profess to be Christians, but are **"the enemies of the cross of Christ."**

> **"For many walk, of whom I have told you often, and now tell you even weeping, that they are the enemies of the cross of Christ: whose end is destruction, whose God is their belly, and whose glory is in their shame, who**

mind earthly things" (Philippians 3:18, 19). These people to whom Paul referred apparently were once partakers of the grace of God in salvation, but by their walk had proved to all who observed them that they were in fact "**enemies of the cross of Christ.**" In any event, all those who so walk give evidence that they are "**enemies of the cross of Christ.**" They are apostates. What are the characteristics of apostates?

1. ***"Whose God is their belly."*** They live by what appeals to the appetites. That which tastes good and feels good becomes for them the criterion by which they decide what is acceptable, what is right or wrong. Then they twist the Scriptures to justify their actions "**unto their own destruction" (2 Peter 3:16).**

2. ***"Whose glory is in their shame."*** Since our first parents sinned in the Garden of Eden, man's body is his shame. Adam knew no shame until his nature was corrupted. After he sinned, he hid himself from God because he was ashamed and afraid. Apostates, due to a seared conscience, know neither shame nor fear before God and man. They appear in public with shamefully exposed bodies. They further accent their shame by bedecking their bodies "**with broided hair, or gold, or pearls, or costly array" (1 Timothy 2:9),** which Paul told Timothy does not become "**women**

professing godliness."

3. ***"Who mind earthly things."*** The great importance they place on earthly things is evidence that they have set their affections upon them. Paul told the Colossian saints:

> **"If ye then be risen with Christ, seek those things which are above, where Christ sitteth on the right hand of God. Set your affection on things above, not on things on the earth. For ye are dead, and your life is hid with Christ in God. When Christ, who is our life, shall appear, then shall ye also appear with him in glory. Mortify therefore your members which are upon the earth; fornication, uncleanness, inordinate affection, evil concupiscence, and covetousness, which is idolatry: for which things' sake the wrath of God cometh on the children of disobedience: in the which ye also walked some time, when ye lived in them" (Colossians 3:1–7).**

The life of the child of God is not wrapped up in material things, sensuous enjoyments, or shameful bodily exposure and display. All of life is lived for the glory of God, with things and the body utilized for His purposes in the advancement of His kingdom on earth. Apostates, on the other hand, have left their relationship of discipleship with Christ and now concern themselves with having a good life on earth with self-seeking, devising pleasures for themselves, and seeking acceptance among men.

GRACE REIGNS THROUGH RIGHTEOUSNESS

In Romans 5:21 we read:

"As sin hath reigned unto death, even so might grace reign through righteousness unto eternal life by Jesus Christ our Lord."

Where sin reigns, there is death. Where grace reigns, there is righteousness, holy living, and separation from the practice of sin. Satan's version of God's grace is a cheap grace that allows men to live in disobedience to God's Word and still believe they are saved. God be merciful to the preachers who thus deceive the hearts of the simple, those who love to have their ears tickled with an escapism from the realities of God's eternal holiness. Men contradict themselves when they speak of the holiness of God and then defy His plain commandments with divers excuses, such as:

"That was for another culture."

"They were having a particular problem at Corinth."

"We must deal redemptively with these people."

God has a plan for dealing redemptively with men. It is that they put away all sin, separate themselves from all that is not in harmony with His Word, and avail themselves of the power He will give them to effect that separation and to be free indeed from all bondage in the inner man through Jesus Christ our Lord.

Paul exhorted and warned the saints in Corinth:

> **"Your glorying is not good. Know ye not that a little leaven leaveneth the whole lump? Purge out therefore the old leaven, that ye may be a new lump, as ye are unleavened. . . . For what have I to do to judge them also that are without? do not ye judge them that are within? But them that are without God judgeth. Therefore put away from among yourselves that wicked person" (1 Corinthians 5:6, 7, 12, 13).**

Sin, if left unchecked, works in the life of the Christian and in the church, the body of Christ, as leaven works in dough. In a short time the whole is leavened. This has happened to many churches. They have tolerated sin because they falsely believe that sin will not separate church members from God. Slowly at first and then more rapidly, sin permeates the whole body, robbing it of the power to keep sin outside. Satan is then master. Through the lusts of the flesh, he rules those churches. They are enemies of the cross of Christ.

Salvation is deliverance from the power of Satan, sin, the world, and the flesh. Paul wrote that "**the gospel of Christ . . . is the power of God unto salvation.**" God offers no hope of eternal life to those who knowingly live in sin, in disobedience to His Word, subject to the world and its dictates.

Paul, in Ephesians 2:8–10, made it clear that we are *saved by grace*, not by works of righteousness that we may do. Only as we trust the sacrifice of our Lord Jesus Christ can we have our sins forgiven and be made free from the power of the flesh, sin, Satan, and the world.

In our salvation we are "**created in Christ Jesus unto good works, which God hath before ordained that we should walk in them.**" *Ordained* does not mean *optional*. The things God has ordained cannot be made optional by man; they stand unchanged. Either man accepts and conforms to them, or he suffers the consequences.

5.

"Shall We Continue in Sin?": Romans 6

In chapter 6 of the Book of Romans, Paul immediately plunged into the problem of sin in the life of the believer by asking the question, "**Shall we continue in sin, that grace may abound?**" We are told by some that the "once saved, always saved" doctrine magnifies the grace of God. But Paul boldly challenged that theoretical position, declaring that what truly magnifies the grace of God is that it keeps us from sin, truly holy and clean before God and men. Holiness of heart, mind, and body is a reality in the true Gospel of Jesus Christ.

Paul answered his own question very abruptly. **"God forbid. How shall we, that are dead to sin, live any longer therein?"** Such a life is unthinkable, untenable.

In the verses that follow, Paul relates the New Birth to the death and resurrection of Christ. The baptism that he discusses here, the baptism of the Holy Spirit, has the effect of crucifying the old sin nature, rendering it powerless to control the believer's thoughts, affections, and will as long as it remains crucified by the power of Christ. In this sense it is a baptism of death. Then by the power of Christ dwelling within the believer in the person of His Holy Spirit, the believer is transformed and made new, conformed to the image and nature of God. This is a baptism of life. By the power of this new life (**"in the likeness of his resurrection"**), the individual now can say no to sin and from henceforth yield his members to God to do His holy will in everything.

> **"Let not sin therefore reign in your mortal body, that ye should obey it in the lusts thereof. . . . For sin shall not have dominion over you: for ye are not under the law, but under grace" (Romans 6:12, 14).**

God makes man responsible to do His will and to refuse to have any part in anything that is not in full harmony with His will as revealed in His Word. He intends that we know the Word and obey it literally, not some man's evaluation or estimation of it. If we are "**under grace,**" then the grace of God enables us to overcome sin in all our temptations.

> "**Know ye** [the saints] **not, that to whom ye yield yourselves servants to obey, his servants ye are to whom ye obey; whether of sin unto death, or of obedience unto righteousness? But God be thanked, that ye were the servants of sin, but ye have obeyed from the heart that form of doctrine which was delivered you. Being then made free from sin, ye became the servants of righteousness. . . . For when ye were the servants of sin, ye were free from righteousness. What fruit had ye then in those things whereof ye are now ashamed? for the end of those things is death. But now being made free from sin, and become servants to God, ye have your fruit unto holiness, and the end everlasting life. For the wages of sin is death; but the gift of God is eternal life through Jesus Christ our Lord" (Romans 6:16–18, 20–23).**

"**Death**" here refers to eternal separation from God. And Paul, by the Holy Spirit, wrote these verses

"to all that be in Rome, beloved of God, called to be saints." What could more clearly, more specifically refute the false doctrine, "once saved, always saved"? The truth is that when a saint or sinner sins, he yields his members as servants to unrighteousness. Then he is **"free from righteousness."** If he refuses to repent, he dies spiritually.

This agrees with the messages of Ezekiel the prophet and of Jesus (Matthew 7:13–29), which we observed earlier. I repeat: The whole tenor of the Scriptures agrees emphatically that God is holy and that to continue in a state of reconciliation with God, men must also be holy in heart and practice.

Holiness is measured by what we do and **"to whom ye yield yourselves servants to obey."** The Scriptures do not allow for the belief that we are holy positionally but sinners in practice. **"His servants ye are to whom ye obey; whether of sin unto death, or of obedience unto righteousness."**

This agrees with Peter's testimony in Acts 5:32. When the apostles were brought into court before the Sanhedrin for their faith and for preaching the Gospel, Peter declared that God gives the Holy Spirit **"to them that obey him."** God sees no righteousness in those who do not obey. He declares the disobedient to be sinners, without hope of eternal life.

"Ye *were* the servants of sin, but ye have obeyed from the heart that form of doctrine which was delivered you." And notice carefully the difference such obedience made in their standing with God. **"But *now* being made free from sin, and become servants to God, ye have your fruit unto holiness, and *the end everlasting life.*"**

Remember, for saint and sinner:

> **"The wages of sin is death; but the gift of God is eternal life through Jesus Christ our Lord."**

The gift is ours when we turn from sin and trust Christ for power to be holy in heart and to manifest holiness in the life that we live.

6.

The Problem of the Will: Romans 7

Romans 7 pictures Paul in a state of distress under the power of sin, in bondage to the sin nature within him. He called it "**the law of sin which is in my members**" and confessed that this bondage was a wretched condition.

What was the problem? Paul identified the problem when he said, "**I am carnal, sold under sin**" **(Romans 7:14).**

It is *the problem of the will.* The carnal nature is anti-God and pressures a person in his intellect (mind) to be selfish, to make demands that will allow this anti-God nature to have its way in his life.

In every conflict in man's life, the problem of the will is involved. It does not seem reasonable to man (to his fleshly nature) to surrender himself to the wishes or commands of another. Authority resides in his own mind. He will decide what he will do in every situation that arises in his life.

The Law of God shows us the exceeding sinfulness of our nature. When we know what we are supposed to do, we find a resistance within that would rather do it another way. Indeed, this resistance takes possession of our being, and we find ourselves doing what we do not want to do.

> **"What shall we say then? Is the law sin? God forbid. Nay, I had not known sin, but by the law: for I had not known lust, except the law had said, Thou shalt not covet. But sin, taking occasion by the commandment, wrought in me all manner of concupiscence** [desire for the forbidden]. **For without the law sin was dead. . . . Wherefore the law is holy, and the commandment holy, and just, and good. Was then that which is good made death unto me? God forbid. But sin, that it might appear sin, working death in me by that which is good; *that sin by the commandment might***

***become exceeding sinful.* For we know that the law is spiritual: but I am carnal, sold under sin. For that which I do I allow not: for what I would, that do I not; but what I hate, that do I. If then I do that which I would not, I consent unto the law that it is good. Now then it is no more I that do it, but sin that dwelleth in me" (Romans 7:7, 8, 12–17).**

Paul, in his own experience, finally cried out:

"O wretched man that I am! who shall deliver me from the body of this death?" (Romans 7:24).

In his mind he had decided to do what he knew to be God's will. But he found himself tied to a nature that was perverse and that overpowered his will. In practice he found himself doing what he really did not want to do. He hated it, but he was in bondage to it.

When men and women experience this conflict repeatedly, they begin to hate themselves. They hate the ones who require of them certain rules that they cannot keep. But this is God's way of bringing man to the end of himself, to the realization of his need of the Saviour, Jesus Christ. In his desperation, man then has the privilege of turning to Jesus, disowning himself (his sinful nature), turning from his own resources, and casting himself wholly on the Lord Jesus. At this point Jesus can move in and deliver him.

But when, for any reason, man decides that God no longer requires obedience to His commandments, he moves away from one of the primary means that God designed to show man his own insufficiency. Man considers that what seems good to him is satisfactory also to God. But God's evaluation of that is:

> **"For my thoughts are not your thoughts, neither are your ways my ways, saith the Lord. For as the heavens are higher than the earth, so are my ways higher than your ways, and my thoughts than your thoughts" (Isaiah 55:8, 9).**

The commandments of Jesus Christ are pivotal. Keeping them proves our love for the Father and the Son. Refusing to keep His commandments proves that we love ourselves and esteem our own will above His will. Jesus said:

> **"If ye keep my commandments, ye shall abide in my love; even as I have kept my Father's commandments, and abide in his love" (John 15:10).**

The man who takes his own way loves neither the

Father nor the Son.

Man's nature is strong, inherently stubborn, sinful in character, and extremely selfish. It is in harmony with Satan, empowered and supported by him. Satan appeals to this sinful nature to generate in man discontent with the will of God. God through His Word seeks to govern man for his eternal good, but this nature in man despises and resents being governed.

For this reason man has, since the time of Adam, sought ways to peace and heaven other than the route of holy living. He is determined to find some way to circumvent God's sovereign rule in his life and still convince himself that he has peace and hope of eternal life.

These are the struggles, the birth pangs, that brought forth the doctrine that once a person is born again, he never again can be lost; that he has an unconditional security that he will be with God forever; and that nothing he does or can do will ever change that. By manufacturing this doctrine, man has convinced himself that he is free from the law of God that requires him to live a holy life and forsake all known sin. Now he need not consider that someday he will face a thrice-holy, sovereign God and answer for what he has done in his daily life and walk. And he charges God with being the author of this perverse doctrine! What a major step in Satan's subtle effort to thwart God's purpose that His people represent His holy character day by day. It is his effort to cause that they with him be cast into the lake of fire to be tormented eternally.

As this doctrine spread over the Christian community throughout the world, the non-Christian society surrounding these Christian professors was also affected. The conscience of society in general has deteriorated until today there is little conscience left to control society. One of the most powerful tools that Satan has used to bring about this decline is this doctrine of irresponsibility toward God and His sovereignty.

In this respect, the outworking of Satan's machinations to date are manifold. He has masterminded the New Age movement and many other religions and organizations that say "We will be gods" and profess to be the savior of mankind. Through the influence of this doctrine of irresponsibility to God, Satan is deceiving many and is destroying true faith in their hearts and lives.

Jesus taught His disciples that this would happen in the end-times.

> **"Take heed that no man deceive you. For many shall come in my name, saying, I am**

Christ; and shall deceive many. . . . For there shall arise false Christs, and false prophets, and shall shew great signs and wonders; insomuch that, if it were possible, they shall deceive the very elect" (Matthew 24:4, 5, 24).

If deception were not possible, such words would take on the form of foolishness and vanity. Men who make claims that the "**elect**" cannot be deceived mock our blessed Lord Jesus.

Many so-called Christians are deceived by their leaders into believing that Romans 7 is a normal Christian experience. But Paul knew better. He cried out, **"O wretched man that I am! who shall deliver me from the body of this death?"** There is no eternal life in that bondage of knowing God's will but not being able to perform it. That is death, spiritual death.

So then, if we are governed by the desires and the demands of the flesh, we serve sin, not God. In Romans 6 Paul declared that such are without righteousness and are not the servants of God.

God gave His commandments to keep His children, after regeneration, from returning to the old life and getting lost in sin. Our surrender to God (the complete giving up of our own wills) is proven only by our response to something we are asked to do that we would prefer not to do, or would prefer to do otherwise. Jesus Christ reigning in our hearts makes it possible to love and do the will of God.

7.

Carnal Versus Spiritual: Romans 8

In Romans 8:1–4, Paul further explains the relationship between grace and the Law.

"There is therefore now no condemnation to them which are in Christ Jesus, who walk not after the flesh, but after the Spirit. For the law of the Spirit of life in Christ Jesus hath made me free from the law of sin and death. For what the law could not do, in that it was weak through the flesh, God sending his own Son in the likeness of sinful flesh, and for sin,

condemned sin in the flesh: that the righteousness of the law might be fulfilled in us, who walk not after the flesh, but after the Spirit."

What was the problem under the Law? The Law made no provision to render man's sin nature (the law of sin and death in our members) powerless. Therefore, man could not live out the righteousness revealed in the Law. Now in Christ Jesus that provision is available. Now we can cease to walk after the flesh (to mind or obey it, to come under it) because we are delivered from the bondage of it. Instead, we can walk after the Spirit, obeying Him as He enlightens our understanding of God's will in His Word.

"For they that are after the flesh [still under the power of it] **do mind the things of the flesh; but they that are after the Spirit the things of the Spirit. For to be carnally minded is death; but to be spiritually minded is life and peace. Because the carnal mind is enmity against God: for it is not subject to the law of God, neither indeed can be. So then they that are in the flesh cannot please God. But ye are not in the flesh, but in the Spirit, if so be that the Spirit of God dwell in you. Now if any man have not the Spirit of Christ, he**

is none of his" (Romans 8:5–9).

The presence of Jesus Christ in the person of His Holy Spirit in our hearts makes the difference. He now is in control. He bears His fruit of "**love, joy, peace, longsuffering, gentleness, goodness, faith, meekness, temperance**" in our hearts and lives.

The Lord Jesus delivers us from the love of sin, "**to be carnally minded.**" Now we have the mind of Christ, "**to be spiritually minded,**" and love the things of truth and heaven. A renewed mind within produces a transformed life without.

> **"Be ye transformed by the renewing of your mind, that ye may prove what is that good, and acceptable, and perfect, will of God" (Romans 12:2).**

But "**the carnal mind is enmity against God: for it is not subject to the law of God, neither indeed can be.**" This is why people cannot obey God. Such a person is a slave to the carnal nature. He has not unreservedly surrendered his will to Jesus Christ. Thus, he does not have the mind of Christ. That which God plainly says in His Word about being perfect before Him and living a holy life is foolishness to him. But for the person who is soundly converted through faith, having made a full surrender of his will to God, "**the kingdom of God is . . . righteousness, and peace, and joy in the Holy Ghost" (Romans 14:17).**

God requires holy living on the part of His saints—saints in practice, not just in standing or theory.

> **"If ye live after the flesh, ye shall die: but if ye through the Spirit do mortify the deeds of the body, ye shall live. For as many as are led by the Spirit of God, they are the sons of God" (Romans 8:13, 14).**

It is our privilege and calling in Christ to trust Him to put our sin nature to death (render it powerless to control us) and to receive Christ into our hearts to live and reign over sin, Satan, and the world. In Him we can be victorious unto the end. And living thus by faith in God's Word, if we sin, "**we have an advocate with the Father, Jesus Christ the righteous.**"

While "**we ourselves groan within ourselves, waiting for the adoption, to wit, the redemption of our body,**" we "**hope for that we see not**" and "**with patience wait for it" (Romans 8:23, 25).** We now have a sure hope in Christ. We are identified with His holiness in this life. Now we can freely say:

> **"If God be for us, who can be against us? He that spared not his own Son, but delivered**

him up for us all, how shall he not with him also freely give us all things? Who shall lay any thing to the charge of God's elect? It is God that justifieth. Who is he that condemneth? It is Christ that died, yea rather, that is risen again, who is even at the right hand of God, who also maketh intercession for us. Who shall separate us from the love of Christ?" (Romans 8:31–35).

8.

Peter Teaches Holiness of Life

> **"Wherefore gird up the loins of your mind, be sober, and hope to the end for the grace that is to be brought unto you at the revelation of Jesus Christ; as obedient children, not fashioning yourselves according to the former lusts in your ignorance: but as he which hath called you is holy, so be ye holy in all manner of conversation; because it is written, Be ye holy; for I am holy" (1 Peter 1:13–16).**

The "**conversation**" that Peter here addresses is our

daily life and practice—what we do with our hands, feet, tongues, and bodies. It is what men see as we live before them. We are to be holy "**in all manner**" of expression that emanates from our being.

Observe carefully that this admonition was given in a setting in which Peter admonished his readers to be ready to meet the Lord and possess their inheritance in glory.

> **"Blessed be the God and Father of our Lord Jesus Christ, which according to his abundant mercy hath begotten us again unto a lively hope by the resurrection of Jesus Christ from the dead, to an inheritance incorruptible, and undefiled, and that fadeth not away, reserved in heaven for you" (1 Peter 1:3, 4).**

Being prepared to take possession of that inheritance depends upon being "**holy in all manner of conversation**" in this life. God requires a holy walk, even in a time of severe persecution, as those to whom Peter wrote were experiencing. Like Paul, Peter filled his epistles with practical helps and commandments to the saints on how they should think, walk, and talk. Let us consider a few.

> **"Seeing ye have purified your souls in**

obeying the truth through the Spirit unto unfeigned love of the brethren, see that ye love one another with a pure heart fervently" (1 Peter 1:22).

Peter explained that this love relationship between the brethren is a result of being born again by the Word of God, which "**endureth for ever.**" The lack of love that is tolerated among church members who live in disobedience to this and many other suchlike commands leaves them unprepared for the Lord's coming.

Consider another of Peter's commands to the saints:

"Dearly beloved, I beseech you as strangers and pilgrims, abstain from fleshly lusts, which war against the soul; having your conversation honest among the Gentiles: that, whereas they speak against you as evildoers, they may by your good works, which they shall behold, glorify God in the day of visitation" (1 Peter 2:11, 12). Following after the devices of the world to gratify the lusts and appetites of the flesh is forbidden to the Christian. Such a life is not acceptable to God. But when men take the view that what one does has no effect on his standing with God and being prepared for the coming of Jesus and the judgment that will follow, then it is easy to follow the world and "**enjoy the pleasures of sin for a season" (Hebrews 11:25).**

Peter commented further on this subject:

> **"For the time past of our life may suffice us to have wrought the will of the Gentiles** [the unregenerate world], **when we walked in lasciviousness, lusts, excess of wine, revellings, banquetings, and abominable idolatries: wherein they think it strange that ye run not with them to the same excess of riot, speaking evil of you: who shall give account to him that is ready to judge the quick and the dead" (1 Peter 4:3–5).**
>
> **"Therefore be ye also ready: for in such an hour as ye think not the Son of man cometh" (Matthew 24:44).**

How will those who revel in shameful immodesty on the beaches or otherwise expose their bodies to the public be prepared to meet our holy Lord Jesus, who is despised by the world that they follow? or those who take license to feed their lusts by watching the shows on TV (including the commercials) or at the theater? or those who participate in or follow dances, public games, and parties with their abominable idolatries? or those who have their affections set on fun and frolic and the pleasures of this world?

Peter also warned the saints to be careful to do certain things to make their calling and election sure.

> **"For if ye do these things, ye shall never fall" (2 Peter 1:10).**

> **"Seeing then that all these things shall be dissolved, what manner of persons ought ye to be in all holy conversation and godliness, looking for and hasting unto the coming of the day of God, wherein the heavens being on fire shall be dissolved, and the elements shall melt with fervent heat? Nevertheless we, according to his promise, look for new heavens and a new earth, wherein dwelleth righteousness" (2 Peter 3:11–13).**

Is this an unconditional promise? No.

> **"Wherefore, beloved, seeing that ye look for such things, be diligent that ye may be found of him in peace, without spot, and blameless. . . . Ye therefore, beloved, seeing ye know these things before, beware lest ye also, being led away with the error of the wicked, fall from your own stedfastness" (2 Peter 3:14, 17).**

9.

The Evidence of Sonship

God has left us some simple tests whereby we can know that we know Him. The Holy Spirit directed the apostle John to record some of these in simple language.

1. Keeping the Commandments of God

"And hereby we do know that we know him, if we keep his commandments. He that saith, I know him, and keepeth not his commandments, is a liar, and the truth is not in him. But whoso keepeth his word, in him verily

is the love of God perfected: hereby know we that we are in him. He that saith he abideth in him ought himself also so to walk, even as he walked" (1 John 2:3–6).

Keeping God's commandments out of a willing heart gives evidence that a person has surrendered the management of his life to the Lord Jesus Christ. There is concrete evidence that from the heart he sincerely believes that "**Jesus Christ . . . is . . . King of kings, and Lord of lords.**" He has voluntarily placed himself under His divine direction and delights in that service.

Further, obeying God's commands provides evidence to those who observe the believer's life that he has repented (in godly sorrow) of his sinful tendencies and acts and has renounced his own sinful nature with its lusts, desires, and motivations.

When believers keep the commandments of God, it shows that they love God. "**And his commandments are not grievous" (1 John 5:3).**

On the other hand, a person who says, "**I know him,**" and does not keep His commandments, gives evidence of two things: (1) "**he . . . is a liar**"; and (2) "**the truth is not in him.**" The prophet Isaiah said that the Lord told him:

"If they speak not according to this word, it is because there is no light in them" (Isaiah 8:20).

God refuses to give understanding of truth to those who do not obey His commandments. Out of their own understanding and reasoning they reach the conclusions that they teach. Let us not think that a man who has a charming personality but does not obey the commandments of God will be able to teach us truth. **"The truth is not in him."**

2. Doing Righteousness

"If ye know that he is righteous, ye know that every one that doeth righteousness is born of him. . . . And every man that hath this hope in him purifieth himself, even as he is pure. . . . In this the children of God are manifest, and the children of the devil: whosoever doeth not righteousness is not of God, neither he that loveth not his brother" (1 John 2:29; 3:3, 10).

Doing that which God says is right is the evidence that our faith in God's Word is genuine, that we have a saving faith. Without saving faith, we are still under the bondage of the sinful nature and hence not able to do right. **"Whosoever doeth not righteousness"** gives evidence that he is not willing or that he does not understand how to appropriate the salvation from sin which Jesus Christ accomplished by His crucifixion and resurrection.

3. *Loving Our Brother*

> **"He that saith he is in the light, and hateth his brother, is in darkness even until now. He that loveth his brother abideth in the light, and there is none occasion of stumbling in him. But he that hateth his brother is in darkness, and walketh in darkness, and knoweth not whither he goeth, because that darkness hath blinded his eyes" (1 John 2:9–11).**

Hatred—a failure to love our brother—produces blindness in the heart in relation to spiritual things. God withholds understanding of Himself and truth when we do not love our brother. Notice that this is stated in the singular—brother, not brethren. The love of God reaches to every soul, without exception.

> **We know that we have passed from death unto life, because we love the brethren. He that loveth not his brother abideth in death. Whosoever hateth his brother is a murderer: and ye know that no murderer hath eternal life abiding in him. . . . If a man say, I love God,**

and hateth his brother, he is a liar: for he that loveth not his brother whom he hath seen, how can he love God whom he hath not seen?" (1 John 3:14, 15; 4:20).

Loving our brother or failing to love him is evidence of our standing with God. If we do not love him, we hate him. The Bible provides no middle ground. The middle ground ("I don't love him, but neither do I hate him") is the product of human reasoning. Satan continually produces halfway positions and uses them to pacify professed Christians in living short of a full surrender that gives Christ control of the entire being and life.

"Love is of God. . . . He that loveth not knoweth not God; for God is love" (1 John 4:7, 8).

"He that loveth not his brother abideth in death" (1 John 3:14).

When the Holy Spirit sheds the love of God abroad in our hearts, then we too love all men and hate none.

"But God commendeth his love toward us, in that, while we were yet sinners, Christ died for us" (Romans 5:8).

The evidence of our heavenly sonship is that we love others as God has loved us. His love in us (the true character of His divine nature) causes us to love those who mistreat us. Jesus teaches us:

> **"Love your enemies, bless them that curse you, do good to them that hate you, and pray for them which despitefully use you, and persecute you; that ye may be the children of your Father which is in heaven: for he maketh his sun to rise on the evil and on the good, and sendeth rain on the just and on the unjust" (Matthew 5:44, 45).**

Numerous verses in the New Testament tell us that we have eternal life by placing our faith (believing) in the Lord Jesus Christ. The verses quoted above help to define what it means to believe on the Lord Jesus Christ. They specify the kind of fruit that is evident in the life of a true believer. They also tell us that the absence of this fruit is evidence that the person **"abideth in death."**

10.

The Testimony of Hebrews

The writer of Hebrews was inspired and directed of God to compare the Old Covenant with the New Covenant. Hence, the Book of Hebrews is often referred to as the book of "better things." Comparisons are made between the Old and New Testaments in respect to

1. The messengers who gave the Covenants
2. The priesthood and its functions
3. The consequence of disobedience and the requirement of faithfulness
4. The threat of sin and unbelief

5. The privileges and responsibilities of the saints
6. The danger of falling away
7. The efficacy of the blood of animals and the blood of Christ
8. The perfection of the sacrifices
9. The perfection of the saints
10. The worldly and the heavenly sanctuaries
11. Man's access to God
12. The permanence of the Covenants

What was God's purpose in making these comparisons?

In setting forth the better privileges offered to man under the New Covenant, the writer emphasized the holiness of God and solemnly warned repeatedly of the consequences if man presumes on that holiness by careless living. Greater privileges bring greater responsibility to be faithful, and greater consequences if man fails to represent in his lifestyle the holiness of God.

A common error in evangelical circles is the idea that we are living "**under grace,**" as though grace was something that, when applied to a person's life, becomes some sort of covering through which God does not see that person's sins, though he may be full of them day by day. Not a shred of evidence in the entire New Testament supports such a view. It is a part of Satan's delusion, the great deception of the latter days.

Let us observe in the Book of Hebrews a few of the comparisons made and the conclusions drawn in the context. We will begin with:

THE MESSENGERS OF THE TWO COVENANTS

Chapter 1 begins with a forceful comparison:

> **"God, who at sundry times and in divers manners spake in time past unto the fathers *by the prophets,* hath in these last days spoken unto us *by his Son,* whom he hath appointed heir of all things, by whom also he made the worlds; who being the brightness of his glory, and the express image of his person, and upholding all things by the word of his power, when he had by himself purged our sins, sat down on the right hand of the Majesty on high; *being made so much better than the angels,* as he hath by inheritance obtained a more excellent name than they" (Hebrews 1:1–4).**

Under the Old Testament, God gave His message to the prophets by the ministry of angels. The prophets served in the time of types and shadows but were not the fulfillment of the perfect covenant God made with man. It was a time of the foreshadowing of the real.

> **"When he bringeth in the firstbegotten into the world, he saith, And let all the angels of God worship him. . . . Who maketh his angels spirits, and his ministers a flame of fire. But unto the Son he saith, Thy throne, O God, is for ever and ever: a sceptre of righteousness is the sceptre of thy kingdom" (Hebrews 1:6–8).**

Chapter 2 then begins with a forceful conclusion to the comparisons made in chapter 1:

> **"Therefore we ought to give the more earnest heed to the things which we have heard, lest at any time we should let them slip. For if the word spoken by angels was stedfast, and *every transgression and disobedience received a just recompence of reward;* how shall we escape, if we neglect so great salvation; which at the first began to be spoken by the Lord, and was confirmed unto us by them that heard him; God also bearing them witness, both with signs and wonders, and with divers miracles, and gifts of the Holy Ghost, according to his own will?" (Hebrews 2:1–4).**

In this passage God is intently showing man that there is obviously no escape if man neglects to obey the Messenger of the New Covenant, Jesus Christ. The implication in much present-day teaching is that since we are under the New Covenant and no longer under the Law, the responsibility of faithful obedience in holy living in heart, mind, spirit, and body is lessened or no longer required. This brings to the fore a false notion of the love of God—that God's great love for us could never be so hard as to require full obedience.

From this notion proceeds the teaching that parents should not punish their children with the rod but should seek other, more gentle (permissive) means to correct their children. The result is many confused, insecure persons, who in mature years constantly and selfishly demand their rights. Unresolvable conflict results from the selfish demands of those who have grown up in this permissive environment. For this reason we witness much divorce, remarriage, and often divorce again.

The New Testament teaches consistently that we are under the law of Christ, which is a higher, more stringent law than that of the Old Covenant. But the New offers with its "**high**" and "**holy calling**" the provisions that make possible its fulfillment in faithful obedience.

> **"That the righteousness of the law might be fulfilled in us, who walk not after the flesh, but after the Spirit" (Romans 8:4).**

Those who submit to the lordship of Christ experience through Him deliverance from the flesh and its will. Such individuals live together in peace and holiness and experience true fellowship in Christ. They constitute the true church of Jesus Christ.

Note carefully the warning in Hebrews 2:3: "**How shall we escape, if we neglect so great salvation . . . ?**" The "**recompence of reward**" in the Old Covenant was severe, and the warning here is that because of the superior Messenger of the New Covenant, the "**recompence of reward**" shall be more severe and more sure. "**So great salvation**" refers to deliverance from sin, as we see in chapter 3.

> **"Take heed, brethren, lest there be in any of you an evil heart of unbelief, in departing from the living God. But exhort one another daily, while it is called To day; lest any of you be hardened through the deceitfulness of sin. For we are made partakers of Christ, if we hold the beginning of our confidence stedfast unto the end" (Hebrews 3:12–14).**

The admonition to the saints is to "**exhort one**

another daily." Why? "**Lest any of you be hardened through the deceitfulness of sin.**" Sin brings death (Romans 6:23). Sin separates people from God (Isaiah 59:2). The true saints of God are concerned about sin in both their own lives and the lives of their brethren because sin is spiritual poison; it kills the spiritual life and separates a man from his God as it did the holy man and woman in the Garden of Eden.

God is a jealous God. His jealousy protects His holiness. He will not have sin dwell in His presence. He will not dwell in the heart of a person who is knowingly tolerating sin in his life. This warning comes clear to us in chapter 4:

> **"Let us therefore fear, lest, a promise being left us of entering into his rest, any of you should seem to come short of it. For unto us was the gospel preached, as well as unto them: but the word preached did not profit them, not being mixed with faith in them that heard it" (Hebrews 4:1, 2).**

In Hebrews 3 we read, "**Lest there be in *any of you* an evil heart of unbelief, in departing from the living God.**" And in Hebrews 4 we read, "**Lest . . . *any of you* should seem to come short of**" the promise. Whom was the writer addressing when he said, *any of you*? It was the "**holy brethren, partakers of the heavenly calling" (Hebrews 3:1).** The holy brethren who are partakers of Christ are in danger of falling away, "**in departing from the living God.**" They can be hardened through the deceitfulness of sin and come under the condemnation of God again.

When men in unbelief do not accept the message of the Scriptures, in which God expressly and pointedly states that He requires from His people holiness in heart, mind, spirit, and body (actions), they are revealing that they despise the holiness of God. From this viewpoint of contempt, they consider obedience to God's Word in all the details of life unnecessary, and continue to live in their sins.

COMPARING THE PRIESTHOOD, SACRIFICES, AND BLOOD OF THE COVENANTS

In chapters 5 through 10:22, the perfection of the priesthood and the sacrifice of Christ and His blood in the New Covenant is compared with the imperfection of the priesthood, sacrifices, and blood in the Old Covenant. The central truth that emerges from this comparison is the weakness and inadequacy of the Old Testament sacrifices to remove or put away sin.

> **"For the law having a shadow of good things to come, and not the very image of the**

things, can never with those sacrifices which they offered year by year continually make the comers thereunto perfect. For then would they not have ceased to be offered? because that the worshippers once purged should have had no more conscience of sins. But in those sacrifices there is a remembrance again made of sins every year. For it is not possible that the blood of bulls and of goats should take away sins. . . . And every priest standeth daily ministering and offering oftentimes the same sacrifices, which can never take away sins" (Hebrews 10:1–4, 11).

The perfection of the priesthood of Christ and the efficacy of His blood stand in sharp contrast to this.

"For Christ is not entered into the holy places made with hands, which are the figures of the true; but into heaven itself, now to appear in the presence of God for us: nor yet that he should offer himself often, as the high priest entereth into the holy place every year with blood of others; for then must he often have suffered since the foundation of the world: but now once in the end of the world hath he appeared to put away sin by the sacrifice of

> **himself. . . . But this man, after he had offered one sacrifice for sins for ever, sat down on the right hand of God; from henceforth expecting till his enemies be made his footstool. For by one offering he hath perfected for ever them that are sanctified. Whereof the Holy Ghost also is a witness to us: . . . and their sins and iniquities will I remember no more. Now where remission of these is, there is no more offering for sin" (Hebrews 9:24–26; 10:12–15, 17, 18).**

The Old Testament sacrifices *covered* the sins of the offerer. "**Blessed are they whose iniquities are forgiven, and whose sins are covered" (Romans 4:7).** God, in offering the perfect sacrifice in His Son, provided for the *taking away* of our sins. This perfect sacrifice was foreshadowed in the animal sacrifices that the Old Testament saints offered in obedience to what God had commanded in the Law that He gave to Moses. The sins that were covered for those saints, who offered their sacrifices believing that the perfect sacrifice would be brought forth by God in His time, were taken away when Christ's blood was shed and accepted by God as the perfect "**propitiation . . . for the sins of the whole world" (1 John 2:2).**

"But Christ being come an high priest of good things to come, by a greater and more perfect tabernacle, not made with hands, that is to say, not of this building; neither by the blood of goats and calves, but by his own blood he entered in once into the holy place, having obtained eternal redemption for us. . . . And for this cause he is the mediator of the new testament, that by means of death, for the redemption of the transgressions that were under the first testament, they which are called might receive the promise of eternal inheritance. . . . And these all, having obtained a good report through faith, received not the promise: God having provided some better thing for us, that they without us should not be made perfect" (Hebrews 9:11, 12, 15; 11:39, 40).

When Jesus' blood was shed and accepted by God in heaven, the true holy of holies, then the sins that were covered by the sacrifices that the saints had offered in faith under the Old Covenant were taken away. Likewise today the sins of the penitent, who put their confidence in the merits of the blood of Jesus, are also taken away.

Hebrews 10 pictures the direct access to the throne

of God that saints now have through the blood of Christ—"**boldness to enter into the holiest.**" Contrast this with the holy of holies in the tabernacle in the wilderness: there the high priest alone could enter once a year, where God met him when he appeared to atone for the sins of all the people. Our High Priest, having taken our sins away, is seated at the right hand of God. He has constant, direct access to the Father and intercedes in our behalf on the merits of His blood, the eternal sacrifice. This makes provision, upon our repentance, for immediate forgiveness and cleansing from any sin we may commit in our walk with God. See 1 John 1:9; 2:1, 2.

The urgent need pressed upon us is to admonish one another, to "**consider one another to provoke unto love and to good works: . . . exhorting one another: and so much the more, as ye see the day approaching.**" This compares with the message we observed in Hebrews 3.

Following the comparison made in Hebrews 1–4 of the messengers of the Covenants, a warning was given to the reader. So also a solemn warning follows the comparison made in chapters 5–10 of the priesthood and sacrifices of the Old and New Testaments, under Law and under grace. Many teach that under grace God is permissive, that He does not take our sins into account. But what say the Scriptures?

> **"For if we sin wilfully after that we have received the knowledge of the truth, there remaineth no more sacrifice for sins, but a certain fearful looking for of judgment and fiery indignation, which shall devour the adversaries. He that despised Moses' law died without mercy under two or three witnesses: of how much sorer punishment, suppose ye, shall he be thought worthy, who hath trodden under foot the Son of God, and hath counted the blood of the covenant, wherewith he was sanctified, an unholy thing, and hath done despite unto the Spirit of grace? For we know him that hath said, Vengeance belongeth unto me, I will recompense, saith the Lord. And again, The Lord shall judge his people. It is a fearful thing to fall into the hands of the living God" (Hebrews 10:26–31).**

We must remember that these words are addressed to the "**holy brethren, partakers of the heavenly calling.**" The "**we**" in the expression "**if *we* sin wilfully**" refers to them and to us who now are saints in the land of the living.

These conclusions are to be believed, not interpreted away in an effort to find some loophole that allows us to escape this accountability. Knowing the will of God, as expressed in His Word, makes us answerable to Him for what we do with that knowledge. Jesus repeatedly taught accountability to God and that those who are unfaithful in that are His enemies. Notice the parables He gave of the talents and the pounds in Matthew 25:14–30 and in Luke 19:13–27.

"If we sin wilfully"—that is, with a knowledge that our conduct is contrary to God's revealed will in His Word—there is no sacrifice that God has provided or can accept to forgive sins under those circumstances. Only when we in godly sorrow repent of those sins and forsake them, with a mind to obey Him henceforth, whatever the cost, is there forgiveness through the blood of Christ Jesus. That alone represents true, saving faith.

The lordship of Christ makes all men accountable to Him. To say that once we are saved we are unconditionally, eternally saved ignores accountability, a central truth of the Gospel. It denies the probationary covenant relationship God designed for mankind.

In the beginning, God placed man on probation. Man's continuing fellowship with **"God walking in the garden in the cool of the day" (Genesis 3:8)** was contingent upon his obedience to God. Adam and Eve broke their covenant with God by eating of the fruit of the tree of which God had said, **"Thou shalt not eat of it" (Genesis 2:17).**

God's covenant with sinful man for his salvation is conditional. The prophet Isaiah stated it in these words:

> **"If ye be willing and obedient, ye shall eat the good of the land: but if ye refuse and rebel, ye shall be devoured with the sword: for the mouth of the Lord hath spoken it" (Isaiah 1:19, 20).**

The passages that we have considered thus far show clearly that man is on trial to test or prove the genuine quality of his faith in God by faithful obedience to the terms of the Gospel.

> **"Even so faith, if it hath not works, is dead, being alone" (James 2:17).**

It is lifeless and powerless, leaving man in bondage to Satan, the lusts of his flesh, and the pleasures and things of this world.

Remember, the blood of Jesus is provided to put sin away, not to cover it. We stand condemned before God for any sin over which we do not have victory. And we are in bondage to that sin.

All that is left for the person who for *any* reason

justifies himself in defeat or takes the liberty to disobey *any* part of the Word of God is "**a certain fearful looking for of judgment and fiery indignation, which shall devour the adversaries.**" The writer of Hebrews wrote this under the inspiration of the Holy Spirit. Who are we to change it?

Then the writer went on to explain how much more serious disobedience is under the New Testament than it was under the Old Testament. "If," he said, "a person who despised Moses' Law by disobeying it died without mercy when his disobedience was verified under two or three witnesses, of how much more severe a punishment would a person be worthy who has despised the message and Law of the Son of God?" Observe carefully how he described or defined disobedience to the commands of Christ.

1. ***"Has trodden under foot the Son of God."*** Disobedience to Christ and His Word entails rejecting His position as Lord of all, His having been made the Head of all things by the Father. The thought here is "to reject with disdain" (*Strong's Concordance, Greek Dictionary*, #2662, p. 40). Christ sees our unwillingness to believe and obey Him as a disdainful rejection of His place at the right hand of God, His position as "**King of kings, and Lord of lords**" in God's domain and in our hearts.

2. ***"Hath counted the blood of the covenant, wherewith he was sanctified, an unholy thing."*** The blood of animals could not take away sins. It covered the sins of the offerer until the perfect sacrifice was offered that took them away.

> **"For the law having a shadow of good things to come, and not the very image of the things, can never with those sacrifices which they offered year by year continually make the comers thereunto perfect. . . . But this man, after he had offered one sacrifice for sins for ever, sat down on the right hand of God. . . . For by one offering he hath perfected for ever them that are sanctified. Whereof the Holy Ghost also is a witness to us" (Hebrews 10:1, 12, 14, 15).**

The blood of Christ was shed to remove sin. It is holy and therefore cannot be associated with sin.

> **"Now the God of peace, that brought again from the dead our Lord Jesus, that great shepherd of the sheep, through the blood of the everlasting covenant, make you perfect in every good work to do his will, working in you that which is wellpleasing in his sight, through Jesus Christ; to whom be glory for ever and**

> **ever" (Hebrews 13:20, 21).**

The "**everlasting covenant**" makes the comers thereunto perfect, working in them holy thoughts and conduct. By the blood of Christ, the inner man is transformed, renewed, and made, "**after the image of him that created him" (Colossians 3:10),** by the "**renewing of the Holy Ghost" (Titus 3:5),** a "**new man, which after God is created in righteousness and true holiness" (Ephesians 4:24).**

> **"But we all, with open face beholding as in a glass the glory of the Lord, are changed into the same image from glory to glory even as by the Spirit of the Lord" (2 Corinthians 3:18).**

This all speaks of holiness of heart, mind, and life if we would be identified with Jesus Christ and be a part of His kingdom.

> **"Follow peace with all men, and holiness, without which no man shall see the Lord" (Hebrews 12:14).**

3. ***"Hath done despite unto the Spirit of grace."*** The Spirit of God is the Holy Spirit. He is the administrator of "**the grace of God that bringeth salvation**" and teaches us "**that, denying ungodliness and worldly lusts, we should live soberly, righteously,**

and godly, in this present world; looking for . . . our Saviour Jesus Christ; who gave himself for us, that he might redeem us from all iniquity, and purify unto himself a peculiar people, zealous of good works" (Titus 2:11–14).

The word *despite* means "contempt, scorn, hatred; contemptuous defiance" (*Funk & Wagnalls Dictionary*). To condone or justify the presence of sin in any form in our lives is to treat the Holy Spirit contemptuously. It is willful disobedience to His promptings, a scorning of the direction He provides from the Word. Such action testifies that we consider Him inferior to ourselves, and His work in our lives undesirable.

Disobedience to God's Word is an insult to His sovereignty, His holiness, and His character. Because Moses and Aaron did not follow God's specific instructions and thus *sanctify God* before the people (Numbers 20:12), and because David and the priests did not sanctify God in the presence of the people, in moving the ark **"not after the due order" (1 Chronicles 15:12–15),** God did not accept their persons and overlook their unbelief. *He openly showed all the people His displeasure with the disobedience of His leaders.*

"Because ye believed me not, to sanctify me in

the eyes of the children of Israel." What was their sin which God regarded so seriously? It was that they leaned to their own understanding and wisdom instead of believing that God's wisdom and instructions were absolute truth and could not be improved upon. When they acted in a way different from what God specifically said, they influenced the people to believe that God is not the absolute God, the Lord God Almighty, perfect in wisdom, the one and only just and holy God. The people were led to believe that God is something less than He truly is, the "**I AM THAT I AM.**"

This truth is little understood by church people. Many ministers and church members are guilty of the same failure: they do not sanctify God in the sight of the people among whom they live. We can be sure that God observes and strongly disapproves of it. *In His own time, He will avenge Himself of this sin as He did with Moses, Aaron, and David.*

> **"For we know him that hath said, Vengeance belongeth unto me, I will recompense, saith the Lord. And again, The Lord shall judge his people. It is a fearful thing to fall into the hands of the living God" (Hebrews 10:30, 31).**

Let the full force of this message sink into your heart. God will judge His people. He will take vengeance on all who defy His sovereignty and holy character by living with known sin in their lives.

Hebrews 12:14–29 once again addresses the significance of the superiority of Jesus' blood, priesthood, and message. The author summarizes the message of the book by saying:

> **"But ye are come unto mount Sion, and unto the city of the living God, . . . and to God the Judge of all, and to the spirits of just men made perfect, and to Jesus the mediator of the new covenant, and to the blood of sprinkling, that speaketh better things than that of Abel" (Hebrews 12:22–24).**

Are we among the **"spirits of just men made perfect"?** Have we **"cleansed ourselves from all filthiness of the flesh *and* spirit, perfecting holiness in the fear of God"?** Are we one with Christ and with God in spirit and in body?

The blood of Abel, crying out from the ground, condemned Cain. But the blood of Jesus cries forgiveness, cleansing, and *deliverance from sin*.

We live in the day when God's plan of redemption from sin has been fulfilled. No longer does God wink at man's weakness and failure. For all who will hear and believe the Gospel message, He has provided forgiveness and cleansing from past sin, and present deliverance from its power.

> **"See that ye refuse not him that speaketh. For if they escaped not who refused him that spake on earth, much more shall not we escape, if we turn away from him that speaketh from heaven: whose voice then shook the earth: but now he hath promised, saying, Yet once more I shake not the earth only, but also heaven. And this word, Yet once more, signifieth the removing of those things that are shaken, as of things that are made, that those things which cannot be shaken may remain. Wherefore we receiving a kingdom which cannot be moved, let us have grace, whereby we may serve God acceptably with reverence and godly fear: for our God is a consuming fire" (Hebrews 12:25–29).**

The cheap grace, or false message of grace, that is preached today in many pulpits, is not the godly grace that is spoken of here. The grace of God is that which enables us to live free of all those things that oppose and offend God. It is the means that God has provided in His plan of redemption whereby we can serve Him in the only way that is acceptable to Him.

It is "**the power of God unto salvation,**" that gift of deliverance from all sin, and the enabling to be fully obedient to all the Word of God.

It is possible to fall from grace (Galatians 5:4). Falling from grace is the failure to appropriate the grace of God to be obedient sons of God, to do all to the glory of God, to continue by grace to be holy. It is trusting in a false plan of salvation, a plan other than that which God has brought to us through His love, mercy, and grace in Christ Jesus our Lord.

The true sons of God are characterized by the fruit of the Spirit in their lives in the home, first of all, and among all men.

> **"The fruit of the Spirit is love, joy, peace, longsuffering, gentleness, goodness, faith, meekness, temperance: against such there is no law" (Galatians 5:22, 23).**

Paul warns that they who live after the flesh and do "**the works of the flesh . . . adultery, . . . uncleanness, . . . hatred, . . . envyings, murders, drunkenness, revellings, and such like . . . shall not inherit the kingdom of God" (Galatians 5:19–21).**

Let us remember that "**it is a fearful thing to fall into the hands of the living God.**"

11.

The Ifs in Salvation

There are many *ifs* in the doctrine of salvation as taught in the New Testament. They express in part the conditions upon which man's salvation hinges. Man must cooperate in fulfilling his part of God's covenant with man. He must give positive evidence of his faith in God and His Word and of the full surrender of his will to God's will.

"For it pleased the Father that in him [Christ] **should all fulness dwell; and, having made peace through the blood of his cross, by**

him to reconcile all things unto himself; by him, I say, whether they be things in earth, or things in heaven. And you, that were sometime alienated and enemies in your mind by wicked works, yet now hath he reconciled in the body of his flesh through death, to present you holy and unblameable and unreproveable in his sight: *if* ye continue in the faith grounded and settled, and be not moved away from the hope of the gospel, which ye have heard" (Colossians 1:19–23).

From this we understand that one who is in the faith can **"move away from the hope of the gospel."** Man's final salvation is conditional on continuing in the faith of the Gospel. Paul's instructions in the rest of the Book of Colossians tell us what is required to **"continue in the faith grounded and settled."**

"Mortify therefore your members which are upon the earth; fornication, uncleanness, inordinate affection, evil concupiscence [the desire in the heart for that which is forbidden], **and covetousness, which is idolatry. . . . But now ye also put off all these; anger, wrath, malice, blasphemy, filthy communication out of your mouth. Lie not one to another, seeing**

that ye have put off the old man with his deeds; and have put on the new man" (Colossians 3:5, 8–10).

Those things must go. The terms "**mortify**" and "**put off**" indicate death and removal, respectively. The natural man reasons that such a strict life is not necessary and would afford no joy. "**But the fruit of the Spirit is . . . joy" (Galatians 5:22).** He *gives* us His joy when the will is fully surrendered to Him. The natural man is void of this understanding, but the spiritually minded receive it by faith in what God says in His Word. "**Through faith we understand" (Hebrews 11:3).**

In Colossians 2:8 Paul further warns us:

"Beware lest any man spoil you through philosophy and vain deceit, after the tradition of men, after the rudiments of the world, and not after Christ."

The reasoning and philosophies of men stem from what man knows about the natural elements and the laws of nature, including his own sinful nature. He compares all that the Bible teaches with that knowledge. His conclusions seem reasonable to him because he makes his comparison with "**the rudiments of the world**" rather than with God and His supernatural holiness, wisdom, and power. In Christ we are made **"partakers of the divine nature, having escaped the corruption that is in the world through lust" (2 Peter 1:4).** As long as men are not delivered from the lusts of their flesh, they interpret the Scriptures and all the circumstances of life in light of their lusts. Until a person is delivered from those lusts, he must reckon with them as a viable factor. He cannot *see* life apart from them. Thus, he is compelled to make room for the lusts of his flesh in all his considerations and conclusions.

Spiritual truths seem foolish to the natural man because he sees no way that he can attain to them. True enough! That is why faith is required to understand both the righteousness of God and how to attain to it.

> **"For the preaching of the cross is to them that perish foolishness; but unto us which are saved it is the power of God" (1 Corinthians 1:18).**
>
> **"But of him are ye in Christ Jesus, who of God is made unto us wisdom, and righteousness, and sanctification, and redemption: that, according as it is written, He that glorieth, let him glory in the Lord" (1 Corinthians 1:30, 31).**

Through faith in Christ, the Christian has been delivered and is continually delivered from the lusts and appetites of the flesh. That leaves him free to consider God's Word and all that it teaches about daily living apart from the demands of the sinful nature. It seems evident that churchmen do not understand (or choose not to believe) that *the faith* teaches us that:

> **"They that are Christ's have crucified the flesh with the affections and lusts" (Galatians 5:24),**

and that:

> **"He that hath suffered in the flesh hath ceased from sin; that he no longer should live the rest of his time in the flesh to the lusts of men, but to the will of God. For the time past of our life may suffice us to have wrought the will of the Gentiles, when we walked in lasciviousness, lusts, excess of wine, revellings, banquetings, and abominable idolatries: wherein they think it strange that ye run not with them to the same excess of riot, speaking evil of you" (1 Peter 4:1–4).**

Many pastors seem satisfied to have their church members *try to imitate* this salvation (deliverance from the flesh and its lusts) instead of trusting Christ for it in reality. The result is men trying to lift themselves (spiritually) by their own bootstraps. Impossible!

> **"Neither is there salvation** [deliverance] **in any other: for there is none other name under heaven given among men, whereby we must be saved" (Acts 4:12).**

Being **"saved"** refers not only to being a member of the family of God positionally, but also to being delivered from the whole system of Satan, the world, and the flesh with its lusts. To have a right standing with God, church members must get out of the world and get the world out of their hearts.

We want to observe two *ifs* in Galatians 5 that are addressed to the saints in Christ Jesus, those who had **"begun in the Spirit" (Galatians 3:3).** One of the *ifs* is in verse 15:

> **"*If* ye bite and devour one another, take heed that ye be not consumed one of another."**

Is Paul not telling us that by sinning in this manner we will destroy the spiritual life, both in ourselves and in our brethren? Sin always brings spiritual death.

The second *if* is found in verse 25:

> **"*If* we live in the Spirit, let us also walk in the Spirit."**

The two go hand in hand. *If* we do not walk in the Spirit, we will not live long in the Spirit.

Romans 8:9–17 contains eight *ifs* that indicate our salvation is conditional. Let us consider two of them.

> **"*If* ye live after the flesh, ye shall die: but *if* ye through the Spirit do mortify the deeds of the body, ye shall live. For as many as are led by the Spirit of God, they are the sons of God."**

If we **"live after the flesh,"** refusing to mortify it, we shall die, and this in spite of having been made a new creature at one time. The **"ye"** was written to the saints that were in Rome (Romans 1:7). Thus we see that the saints will die spiritually *if* they **"live after the flesh,"** *if* they do not do the things that are pleasing to God.

But *if* the Spirit of God dwells in us, men will see Him bear His fruit as evidence of His presence and control. We will be led by Him in obedience to the Word, which is further evidence of His indwelling and control of all in our lives.

> **"*If* any man have not the Spirit of Christ, he is none of his."**

The lack of the evidence of the Holy Spirit's presence and work in our lives means He is not present. No evidence that we may claim as proof that the Spirit of God dwells in us is valid *if* His fruit is not evident in our daily relationships and *if* we are not obedient to the Word.

12.

"The Ways of Death"

"There is a way which seemeth right unto a man, but the end thereof are the ways of death" (Proverbs 14:12). The "**way which seemeth right unto a man**" is not measured by God's holiness. It is something less, often much less, than the plan of redemption and salvation that God has designed for sinful man, that he might be transformed and thus be a holy creature. By this provision in Christ, God reconciles man to Himself. But to those who are not thus prepared to dwell with Him in heaven, Jesus will say, **"Depart from me, ye that work iniquity" (Matthew 7:23).**

What is iniquity, but disobeying the commands of the Bible? Many churches today are full of disobedience. Women, for example, cut their hair and go about with their heads uncovered. They work outside the home instead of being keepers at home to provide a godly atmosphere for their husbands and children. Men and women dress in the height of fashion, with their bodies uncovered or exposed through tight-fitting clothing, thus promoting the sex craze and immorality of the age. **"The daughters of Zion are haughty" (Isaiah 3:16),** bedecking their bodies with rings, bracelets, chains, pins, changeable suits of apparel (changing with the fashions)—all of which are expressions of pride. Men and women chase after worldly entertainments that gratify and feed the flesh. Many, including some ordained ministers, live in the sins of uncleanness, sex perversion, and/or adultery. Numerous church members are in bondage to their lusts of smoking, drinking, dancing, anger, variance, debate, covetousness, jealousy, bitterness, envy, deceit, whisperings, backbiting, pride, and watching TV and other theatrical performances that militate against and destroy the spiritual life and appetite. Disobedience to parents, church leaders, and the laws of the state is rife. Idolatry, witchcraft, heresies, hatred, theft, extortion, filthy speech, and cursing abound. Paul listed these sins and others in his epistles to the Corinthians, Galatians, Romans, and Ephesians and warned them (and us) that "**they which do such things shall not inherit the kingdom of God.**" (See Romans 1:18–32; 1 Corinthians 6:9, 10; Galatians 5:19–21; Ephesians 5:3–7.)

WILL GOD OVERLOOK THE SINS THAT CHURCH MEMBERS COMMIT?

"And the times of this ignorance God winked at; but now commandeth all men every where to repent: because he hath appointed a day, in the which he will judge the world in righteousness by that man whom he hath ordained; whereof he hath given assurance unto all men, in that he hath raised him from the dead" (Acts 17:30, 31).

Jesus' last message to the church is given in Revelation 22, beginning with verse 12:

"Behold, I come quickly; and my reward is with me, to give every man according as his work shall be. I am Alpha and Omega, the beginning and the end, the first and the last. Blessed are they that *do* his commandments,

that they may have right to the tree of life, and may enter in through the gates into the city. For without are dogs, and sorcerers, and whoremongers, and murderers, and idolaters, and whosoever loveth and maketh a lie. I Jesus have sent mine angel to testify these things in the churches."

Who are the "**dogs**"? Those who "**turn to** [their] **own vomit again" (2 Peter 2:22).** They were once washed and had given up their sins but have now returned to them.

Who are the "**sorcerers**"? Those who turn to mediums with familiar spirits and become involved with witchcraft, astrology, and various occult activities, such as the Ouija board. They cooperate with Satan in his works and worship and are the enemies of God. God will *not* share His honor with His enemies.

Who are the "**whoremongers**"? They are sex perverts, adulterers, fornicators, homosexuals, lesbians, and suchlike.

"Marriage is honourable in all, and the bed undefiled: but whoremongers and adulterers God will judge" (Hebrews 13:4).

Flee from uncleanness and the adulterous marriage.

Repent of the sin, and look to God and His Word to lead you into a life of holiness and purity. Sinning persons will be on the outside of Christ's kingdom.

Jesus said, **"What I say unto you I say unto all, Watch" (Mark 13:37).** But instead of watching to keep themselves ready to meet Jesus in peace by keeping themselves in the Word and love of God (**"This is the love of God, that we keep his commandments" (1 John 5:3)**, many church members watch the world and ape it. A common attitude among such people is "What's wrong with it?" To watch in the sense that Jesus addressed is to ask, **"Lord, what wilt Thou have me to do?"** "What is right about this? What do the Bible and the faithful church say about it? Will it strengthen me in the faith and keep me from evil and in the will of God? Will it keep me separated from the world and its follies? Will it be the right example of the believers and help others to be faithful to God?"

The deceptive belief that once we are saved we are always saved produces much vain reasoning, such as "God is a loving God and surely does not require that we suffer for righteousness' sake." Indeed, in their walk such people avoid the righteousness of God which would bring them into conflict with those who disobey God in the churches. The religious professors who were disobedient to God were the ones from whom Jesus, the apostles, the faithful Anabaptists in the 1500s, and all the faithful martyrs for the Gospel's sake met their opposition and at whose hands they suffered.

Many today, in the uncertainty of their standing with God and the insecurity they experience regarding their future, are turning to extrasensory experiences to find reality. They seek a manifestation of God's presence and blessing in their lives. And Satan, taking full advantage, rewards them with gifts and with revelations, many of which are contrary to what the Bible plainly says; and with assurances in the "Spirit." But often the fruit of the Spirit of God is clearly lacking in their lives. There is no love for truth and no desire to have their lives corrected by the Word of God. When they are approached with what the Word plainly says, they brush it aside and justify their practice.

Any supernatural manifestation that men experience when they ignore the plain commandments of God, refusing to hear them or considering them unimportant for whatever reason, is not of God. It is of Satan. We need not hesitate to believe or declare this as truth, because the Bible says it plainly. What God says stands despite the claims of men that their experience or study teaches them otherwise. Man's experience is never a basis upon which to decide **"What is truth?"** From the beginning of time, God has rejected all such claims. He has always insisted that men accept what He says and reject their own reasoning and experience.

Here is where men either walk *with* God or walk *away from* God. When men are willing to listen to anything that is contrary to what God says in His Word, deciding that what man says sounds reasonable and more to their liking, Satan steps in and readily deceives them. (See 2 Timothy 4:3.)

THE SPIRIT OF ANTICHRIST

In the end-time the Antichrist, by the power that Satan gives him, is going to deceive many.

> **"Even him, whose coming is after the working of Satan with all power and signs and lying wonders, and with all deceivableness of unrighteousness in them that perish; *because they received not the love of the truth, that they might be saved. And for this cause* God shall send them strong delusion, that they should believe a lie: that they all might be damned who believed not the truth, but had pleasure in unrighteousness" (2 Thessalonians 2:9–12).**

The spirit of Antichrist is already at work, manifesting itself in these very areas among those who are not willing to receive the truth. Satan is dangling every imaginable counterfeit of truth before the churches to draw their attention away from exactly what the Bible says on the problems man encounters. Our willingness or unwillingness to believe exactly what God says and to respond favorably to it is what determines whether God continues to protect us from Satan's efforts to deceive us. God is very jealous of His holiness, and He refuses to cooperate with Satan in his doctrine and the compromising practices that he promotes in the hearts and lives of men.

> **"God is jealous, and the Lord revengeth. . . . Who can stand before his indignation? and who can abide in the fierceness of his anger? his fury is poured out like fire, and the rocks are thrown down by him" (Nahum 1:2, 6).**

Yes, **"God *is* love."** But God is also just and jealous for His holy character. He is absolute truth. He extends His mercy and grace to work in us those same qualities of holiness.

13.

The Call to Separation

Sin affects the church like leaven. It spreads throughout the whole body. To the Corinthian brethren, Paul expressed his amazement that they did not understand this.

> **"Know ye not that a little leaven leaveneth the whole lump? Purge out therefore the old leaven, that ye may be a new lump, as ye are unleavened. . . . But them that are without God judgeth. Therefore put away from among yourselves that wicked person" (1 Corinthians**

Paul admonished the Thessalonians:

> **"Now we command you, brethren, in the name of our Lord Jesus Christ, that ye withdraw yourselves from every brother that walketh disorderly, and not after the tradition which he received of us. . . . And if any man obey not our word by this epistle, note that man, and have no company with him, that he may be ashamed" (2 Thessalonians 3:6, 14).**

The only place for sin is on the outside of the church. Christ died to purify, cleanse, purge, and separate us from sin—forgiving our past sins and delivering us from sin in our present experience.

Many so-called evangelical churches do not put sin out of the body as the New Testament instructs, but are fast becoming the **"hold of every foul spirit" (Revelation 18:2).** The doctrine of "once saved, always saved"—this hell-born doctrine that is damning multitudes to eternal torment—has been one of Satan's most effective tools to bring these churches to such a deplorable condition. When preachers and their people believe this doctrine, disciplining disobedient members to put sin out of the body seems much too harsh. Their own love for sin and the ways of the world finds shelter in this Satanic doctrine. Thus, they rob themselves of the discernment of the Holy Spirit, who dwells only with those who obey God. (See Acts 5:32.) He is the Spirit of truth (John 14:16, 17; 15:26) and does not dwell with those who are not strictly honest with truth. The lack of His fruit in their lives is further witness that they do not know Him or possess Him in their lives. The fruit of the Holy Spirit and a willing obedience to the commandments of God, not some miracle-working power or some emotional experience, are the evidence of the Spirit's presence in a person's heart.

> **"The fruit of the Spirit is love, joy, peace, longsuffering, gentleness, goodness, faith, meekness, temperance** [control]" **(Galatians 5:22, 23).**

Repentance, not self-justification, is God's message from cover to cover in His Word. God will punish sinning people "**with everlasting destruction**" unless they sincerely repent with godly sorrow in their hearts. Such repentance is forthcoming when men tremble at God's Word. When they know what He says, they will at once turn from everything in their lives that the Word condemns.

> **"For . . . this selfsame thing, that ye sorrowed after a godly sort, what carefulness it**

wrought in you, yea, *what clearing of yourselves,* yea what indignation, yea, *what fear,* yea, what vehement desire, yea, what zeal, yea, what revenge! *In all things ye have approved yourselves to be clear in this matter*" (2 Corinthians 7:11).

The only saving faith is the faith that responds thus to what God says. This is the evidence of godliness, of godly character, of divine sonship, of Jesus Christ living and reigning in our hearts. This is how all men can tell that God dwells within our hearts. The evidence is in bearing the fruit of the Spirit in our lives and in being obedient to His Word because we love God and His commandments. This is the acid test.

Professing Christians who live contrary to what they know the Bible teaches are mocking God; they are saying they do not believe He means just what He says.

"Be not deceived; God is not mocked: for whatsoever a man soweth, that shall he also reap. For he that soweth to his flesh shall of the flesh reap corruption; but he that soweth to the Spirit shall of the Spirit reap life everlasting" (Galatians 6:7, 8).

Many such church members sow to the flesh by

not keeping their business commitments and marriage vows. They are dishonest and indulge in many sensual enjoyments. God says they "**shall of the flesh reap corruption.**" Jesus will say to them in the last day, "**I never knew you: depart from me, ye that work iniquity" (Matthew 7:23).** Jesus never knew them because they did not relate properly to sin. To them, sin was not the deadly element that separates man from God. Therefore, they did not "**cleanse** [themselves] **from all filthiness of the flesh and spirit.**" The condition for receiving the Holy Spirit is the complete surrender of the will to Jesus Christ, desiring with all the heart that He shall rule over all of life.

> **"He that hath the Son hath life; and he that hath not the Son of God hath not life" (1 John 5:12).**
>
> **"Whosoever he be of you that forsaketh not all that he hath, he cannot be my disciple" (Luke 14:33).**

These are Jesus' own words. Will we say any less? Dare we risk coming to the Judgment where He will be judge, having lived with any other or lesser commitments in life?

> **"For the great day of his wrath is come;**

and who shall be able to stand?" (Revelation 6:17).

According to Revelation 6:12–16, the greatest and most powerful shall not be able to stand. Neither those with the largest following.

The Holy Spirit presents an urgent appeal to the faithful to separate themselves from the apostate church system that tolerates sin and sinners.

"Come out of her, my people, that ye be not partakers of her sins, and that ye receive not of her plagues. For her sins have reached unto heaven, and God hath remembered her iniquities" (Revelation 18:4, 5).

God promises blessings to those who are faithful, obey Him, and overcome Satan to the end. But the warnings that the disobedient will be rejected by God in eternity continue to the end of the New Testament. They constitute a loud call to separation from sin.

"He that overcometh shall inherit all things; and I will be his God, and he shall be my son. But the fearful, and unbelieving, and the abominable, and murderers, and whoremongers, and sorcerers, and idolaters, and all liars, shall have their part in the lake which burneth with fire and brimstone: which is the

second death. . . . Blessed are they that do his commandments, that they may have right to the tree of life, and may enter in through the gates into the city. For without are dogs, and sorcerers, and whoremongers, and murderers, and idolaters, and whosoever loveth and maketh a lie" (Revelation 21:7, 8; 22:14, 15).

Several warnings and instructions in Revelation 22 are of special significance in regard to the call to separation:

"Behold, I come quickly: blessed is he that keepeth the sayings of the prophecy of this book. . . . Behold, I come quickly; and my reward is with me, to give every man according as his work shall be. . . . I Jesus have sent mine angel to testify unto you these things in the churches. . . . The Spirit and the bride say, Come."

Jesus' message to the church in Smyrna testified of their faithfulness. His concluding admonition to them contains a solemn warning and a blessed promise for us:

"Be thou faithful unto death, and I will give thee a crown of life" (Revelation 2:10).

14.

The Security of the Sheep

The tenth chapter of the Gospel of John is a stronghold for those who believe that once a person is saved he can never or will never be lost again. Let us look at this chapter in light of the message we have observed earlier.

Jesus Himself is the good shepherd. He testifies:

> **"I am come that they might have life, and that they might have it more abundantly. I am the good shepherd: the good shepherd giveth his life for the sheep" (John 10:10, 11).**

Jesus left no stone unturned to make adequate provision that we need never fail in the Christian warfare against Satan, the flesh, the world, and sin.

In John 10:28, 29, Jesus promised eternal security for the sheep. It is based on God's sovereign power. While God keeps them, no one is able to pluck them out of His hand. It is important that we also include verse 27 in our consideration of these verses.

> **"My sheep hear my voice, and I know them, and they follow me: and I give unto them eternal life; and they shall never perish, neither shall any man pluck them out of my hand. My Father, which gave them me, is greater than all; and no man is able to pluck them out of my Father's hand."**

Jesus is telling us here, as in other passages, that *if we meet the conditions*, there is absolute protection and security for us. What are the terms of the covenant stated in this passage?

1. ***"My sheep hear my voice."*** An obedient heart will hear when the Master speaks. No word will be ignored. Notice verse 26 of the same chapter: **"But ye believe not, because ye are not of my sheep, as I said unto you."** A distinct mark that separates the true sheep from the false is that those who are truly His sheep hear His voice.

2. ***"And they follow me."*** Not only do they hear His voice, but they do as He bids them. When Jesus called His disciples, He said, "**Follow me.**" They followed in His footsteps, forsaking their own purposes in this life to fulfill His.

> **"And when he putteth forth his own sheep, he goeth before them, and the sheep follow him: for they know his voice" (John 10:4).**

Jesus likens His followers to sheep because they know the voice of their master and respond to it.

3. ***"And a stranger will they not follow, but will flee from him: for they know not the voice of strangers" (John 10:5).***

When church members are obviously getting their lifestyle from the world, whom are they following? Not Jesus Christ. They are following the world. And the world is His enemy.

Paul teaches the same truth. In the first eleven chapters of the Book of Romans, he teaches us of the provisions in God's great plan of salvation through His grace. As he opens chapter 12, he refers to these provisions as "**the mercies of God.**" In the remaining verses of chapter 12, Paul appeals to us to live a life that expresses these mercies, not the lusts and vanities of the world.

"And be not conformed to this world: but be ye transformed by the renewing of your mind, *that ye may prove* what is that good, and acceptable, and perfect, will of God" (Romans 12:2).

In the Book of Ephesians, Paul admonishes us:

"For ye were sometimes darkness, but now are ye light in the Lord: *walk as children of light*" (Ephesians 5:8).

In the second epistle to the Corinthians, Paul explains this truth in greater detail.

"For what fellowship hath righteousness with unrighteousness? and what communion hath light with darkness? And what concord hath Christ with Belial? or what part hath he that believeth with an infidel? And what agreement hath the temple of God with idols? for ye are the temple of the living God; as God hath said, I will dwell in them, and walk in them; and I will be their God, and they shall be my people. Wherefore come out from among them, and *be ye separate,* saith the Lord, and touch not the unclean thing [or person]**; and I will receive you, and will be a Father unto you, and ye shall be my sons and**

daughters, saith the Lord Almighty" (2 Corinthians 6:14–18).

There are specific conditions upon which God will be our God, and upon which we can be His children. God is not changeable; neither are His law and the terms of His covenant with man negotiable.

"I am the Lord, I change not" (Malachi 3:6).

"I AM THAT I AM" (Exodus 3:14).

Our security is in Jesus Christ, the eternal Son of God.

"For all the promises of God in him are yea, and in him Amen, unto the glory of God by us" (2 Corinthians 1:20).

Does it matter then what we do? Does it have any bearing on our eternal destiny? on our relationship with God? It obviously does. And this agrees well with all the rest of the Scriptures.

When the sheep know Jesus, hear His voice, and follow (obey) Him, then He keeps them from evil. **"Neither shall any man pluck them out of my hand."** Man cannot separate us from God. But our own sins can and will.

The message in Romans 8:28–39 likewise assures us that no man or circumstance can separate us from God and His love. But the first part of the chapter is quite specific and emphasizes that when men have carnal minds and live after the flesh, they die spiritually. And if they can die, we know that they had been alive. Men are made alive in Christ Jesus when they repent of their sins, confess them to God, and receive Jesus Christ into their hearts to reign there. And then the warning is that if they go back and live in sin again, they will once more be of the world and its corruption, separated from God. And unless they repent, they will perish with the wicked in the lake of fire and brimstone, with the devil, the beast, and the false prophet. **"And the smoke of their torment ascendeth up for ever and ever."**

However, if we continue faithful to our commitment, to the covenant we have made with our God, He will keep us, and no one can separate us from Him now or ever. Observe again:

> **"And you, that were sometime alienated and enemies in your mind by wicked works, yet now hath he reconciled in the body of his flesh through death, to present you holy and unblameable and unreproveable in his sight: *if ye continue in the faith grounded and settled, and be not moved away from the hope of the gospel*, which ye have heard" (Colossians 1:21–23).**

Again, the terms are conditional. Let us not fail to observe that one can be **"moved away from the hope of the gospel."**

Paul listed a number of sins and then warned the saints at Ephesus:

> **"Let no man deceive you with vain words: for because of these things cometh the wrath of God upon the children of disobedience. Be not ye therefore partakers with them" (Ephesians 5:6, 7).**

If this does not mean that the saints could lose their salvation by being partakers of the sins of the wicked world, then it means nothing. There could be no purpose to such writing, such warning. See also Colossians 3:5, 6; Ephesians 2:2, 3; Titus 2:11–15; 3:3.

Jesus Christ overcame the world and Satan when He lived on earth. He **"gave himself for us, that he might redeem us from all iniquity, and purify unto himself a peculiar people, zealous of good works" (Titus 2:14).**

Beware of false prophets who would teach you otherwise. They will perish in their own doctrine and drown themselves and others in perdition.

> **"But, beloved, we are persuaded better things of you, and *things that accompany***

***salvation* . . . And we desire that every one of you do shew the same diligence to the full assurance of hope unto the end: that ye be not slothful, but followers of them who through faith and patience inherit the promises" (Hebrews 6:9, 11, 12).**

15.

The Sovereign God and Covenant Relationships

God is complete in Himself. He is perfect in wisdom and power. He designs and executes at will. No power or person in existence or that ever will be in existence can interfere with God's sovereign will and purpose.

God: "The self-existent and eternal creator, sustainer, and ruler of life and the universe."*

Sovereign: "One in whom the supreme power . . . is vested; an individual . . . having supreme authority; free, independent, and in no way limited by external authority or influence."*

God testifies to His sovereignty:

> **"Know therefore this day, and consider it in thine heart, that the Lord he is God in heaven above, and upon the earth beneath: there is none else" (Deuteronomy 4:39).**
>
> **"I am the Lord, and there is none else, there is no God beside me: . . . that they may know from the rising of the sun, and from the west, that there is none beside me. I am the Lord, and there is none else. I form the light, and create darkness: I make peace, and create evil: I the Lord do all these things" (Isaiah 45:5–7).**
>
> **"For thine is the kingdom, and the power, and the glory, for ever. Amen" (Matthew 6:13).**

A problem arises in the minds of some as to the sovereignty of God in relation to the free will of man. Since God is sovereign and seeks counsel from none, does not God then decide sovereignly who will be saved?

God created man holy, without sin and corruption in his nature or mind. He also created him a free

*Definitions taken from *Funk and Wagnalls Standard College Dictionary*

moral agent. Within that scope, man can make his own choices, whether he will worship God and obey Him. God desires to have a part of His creation worship Him out of personal choice because of personal belief in His perfect, glorious, resourceful Person. God created man for this purpose. And He has revealed Himself to man sufficiently to provide a satisfactory basis for that choice.

> **"Thou art worthy, O Lord, to receive glory and honour and power: for thou hast created all things, and for thy pleasure they are and were created" (Revelation 4:11).**

God placed the first man and woman in the beautiful Garden of Eden. There He gave man a choice when He issued the first command:

> **"And the Lord God commanded the man, saying, Of every tree of the garden thou mayest freely eat: but of the tree of the knowledge of good and evil, thou shalt not eat of it: for in the day that thou eatest thereof thou shalt surely die" (Genesis 2:16, 17).**

Under this arrangement, Satan also has access to man. Genesis 3 gives the account how man chose to believe Satan and follow his advice, with the result that man died spiritually in his relationship to God.

Since that day, all children inherit from their parents a sinful nature that is anti-God. Like Satan, it is rebellious toward the sovereign rule of God. Jesus expressed it well in one of His parables when the servants of a certain nobleman said, **"We will not have this man to reign over us" (Luke 19:14).**

Satan is God's archenemy. His efforts have consistently been to turn man away from God to serve him, Satan. A chief approach is to lead man to think that God is treating him unfairly. He would have man think that he can be his own god. But it is a deceitful tactic because God did not create man with the ability to meet his own needs. He must rely on a spiritual being that has much greater wisdom and power than he possesses. He has a choice between two, God or Satan. He will be ruled by one or the other.

So man is on probation—a period of time allotted to a man to prove his willingness to live by the terms of God's covenant with him. He must choose whom he will serve.

Since the Fall of man, man is sinful, rebellious, self-willed. But God has devised a plan by which He can transform man, his nature, affections, and conduct, so that he may once again become the very image of his Creator and serve Him in holiness all the days of his life.

Zacharias, the father of John the Baptist, prophesied of the coming of Jesus, who brought this great redemption:

> **"To perform the mercy promised to our fathers, and to remember his holy covenant; the oath which he sware to our father Abraham, that he would grant unto us, that we being delivered out of the hand of our enemies might serve him without fear, in holiness and righteousness before him, all the days of our life" (Luke 1:72–75).**

Our God who created the heavens and the earth, who sustains them and holds their eternal destiny in His hands, has the sovereign right to determine the terms of the covenant by which He will accept a relationship with those whom He has created. The whole of both the Old and the New Testaments is given unto man to make clear the terms of the covenant that God offers to all men.

> **"The gospel of Christ . . . is the power of God unto salvation to every one that believeth. . . . For therein is the righteousness of God revealed from faith to faith: as it is written, The just shall live by faith. For the wrath of God is revealed from heaven against all**

ungodliness and unrighteousness of men" (Romans 1:16–18).

God in His sovereignty and perfect wisdom will not overrule His sovereign plans and decrees. And man is now in the position to choose God's holiness or to perish with the unholy where they shall "**be tormented with fire and brimstone in the presence of the holy angels, and in the presence of the Lamb: and the smoke of their torment ascendeth up for ever and ever: and they have no rest day nor night" (Revelation 14:10, 11).**

Dear Friend, when out of an honest and good heart I decide that God means what He says, that He has every right to set qualifying terms for the receiving of His gifts (including salvation), that by His grace I will repent of my pride in trying to decide what God means by what He says, and that from now on I will endeavor to obey Him implicitly in all that His Word says, I am not in any measure trying to earn the great gift of eternal life.

When men are chosen to receive a large prize in a sweepstakes, they must meet qualifying terms if they would claim it. Often it is so small a matter as presenting a ticket. Failing to do that, they forfeit their right to the gift. By presenting the ticket, are they earning the prize? We surely agree that they are not.

They are meeting the qualifying terms of the giver.

Jesus explains it this way:

"So likewise ye, when ye shall have done all those things which are commanded you, say, We are unprofitable servants: we have done that which was our duty to do" (Luke 17:10).

The time will come when, as Jesus foretold:

"He that is unjust, let him be unjust still: and he which is filthy, let him be filthy still: and he that is righteous, let him be righteous still: and he that is holy, let him be holy still. And, behold, I come quickly; and my reward is with me, to give every man according as his work shall be. I am Alpha and Omega, the beginning and the end, the first and the last" (Revelation 22:11–13).

"He which testifieth these things saith, Surely I come quickly. Amen. *Even so, come, Lord Jesus*" (Revelation 22:20).

16.

Moral Decadence in Society—Who Is to Blame?

Who is responsible for the moral decadence in society throughout the world? The unbelieving churches that no longer believe that God requires holiness of His people are responsible. These same people blame the government, the educational system, capitalism, and many other isms.

Jesus said that Christians are "**the light of the world**" and "**the salt of the earth.**" But the churches have lost their savor. As salt that loses its savor is of no benefit, so the churches have lost the power of God and the message of truth. Failing to serve God's purpose of preservation through believing, living, and proclaiming God's righteousness, they are a leavening influence in society, turning men away from the principles of right conduct in God's Word. Such churches are no longer a blessing in the world but a curse.

> **"A wonderful and horrible thing is committed in the land; the prophets prophesy falsely, and the priests bear rule by their means; and my people love to have it so: and what will ye do in the end thereof?" (Jeremiah 5:30, 31).**

Due to the unfaithfulness of preachers in the pulpit and preachers and members in daily living, many are turned away from God, believing that Christianity is an absurd failure.

As the consciences of the church leaders and members become seared, the conscience of society in general becomes dull and nonfunctioning. The fear of God no longer exists in men's hearts. They sin without fearing the consequences. Thus, society in general is corrupted by an increasing disregard for the laws of God, **"serving divers lusts and pleasures."**

Who is to blame? God has designed the social order with man as the head. In the home, the church, the school, the state, and in all of society, God holds man responsible to maintain purity and right standards of living. Headship involves the right to command with authority. But most men no longer accept that responsibility. People more and more refuse to be ruled. Then Satan takes full advantage of the situation.

God, who made the heavens and the earth, is Sovereign God. All authority on earth resides in Him. He has established laws in His Word that cannot be ignored without suffering the consequences. When these laws are disregarded and man operates according to his own mind and reasoning, the course is always downward, for Satan controls every mind that is not deliberately subject to God. The end is destruction and eternal suffering of the vengeance of God.

Weak, spineless men in the home and church will someday answer to God for their unwillingness to assume the responsibility that God has placed upon them. There is no escape, though men seek it through numerous channels of their own invention, even to the point of divorce and suicide. Such selfish individualism God will call to account on the Judgment Day.

"The day of the Lord is great and very terrible; and who can abide it?" (Joel 2:11).

17.

A Prepared Place for a Prepared People

God's plan of redemption for man includes an eternal abode. God's presence and work of grace in our lives are but a foretaste of what He has prepared for us.

"Ye were sealed with that holy Spirit of promise, which is the earnest of our inheritance until the redemption of the purchased possession, unto the praise of his glory" (Ephesians 1:13, 14).

Jesus comforted and encouraged His disciples by

frequent reference to that which awaits the faithful after this life.

> **"Let not your heart be troubled: ye believe in God, believe also in me. In my Father's house are many mansions: if it were not so, I would have told you. I go to prepare a place for you. And if I go and prepare a place for you, I will come again, and receive you unto myself; that where I am, there ye may be also. . . . I am the way, the truth, and the life: no man cometh unto the Father, but by me" (John 14:1–3, 6).**

What comfort! God has provided a blessed home in eternity with Him in the presence of absolute holiness—in the absence of all sin.

Who is going to dwell there? Peter, Paul, and John are careful to tell us.

Peter identifies heaven as a place "**wherein dwelleth righteousness.**" On the basis of this truth and that the corruptible earth shall be dissolved, he urges that we live in a prepared state to occupy God's sinless abode prepared for His children.

> **"Seeing then that all these things shall be dissolved, what manner of persons ought ye to be in all holy conversation and godliness,**

looking for and hasting unto the coming of the day of God, wherein the heavens being on fire shall be dissolved, and the elements shall melt with fervent heat? Nevertheless we, according to his promise, look for new heavens and a new earth, wherein dwelleth righteousness. Wherefore, beloved, seeing that ye look for such things, be diligent that ye may be found of him in peace, without spot, and blameless" (2 Peter 3:11–14).

Paul emphasizes that the Lord Jesus Christ is preparing for Himself a *holy* bride.

"Christ also loved the church, and gave himself for it; that he might sanctify and cleanse it with the washing of water by the word, that he might present it to himself a glorious church, not having spot, or wrinkle, or any such thing; but that it should be holy and without blemish" (Ephesians 5:25–27).

John had a vision of the new, holy city. He devotes a goodly portion of the closing chapters of the Book of Revelation to explain the requirements for entering this holy, eternal home. After death, there will be no opportunity for preparations. The right to enter the city and live forever in God's presence will be based on having kept the commandments of God, **"according as his work shall be."**

> **"And I saw a new heaven and a new earth: for the first heaven and the first earth were passed away and there was no more sea. And I John saw the holy city, new Jerusalem, coming down from God out of heaven, prepared as a bride adorned for her husband. . . . And there shall in no wise enter into it any thing that defileth, neither whatsoever worketh abomination, or maketh a lie: but they which are written in the Lamb's book of life. . . . And he saith unto me, Seal not the sayings of the prophecy of this book: for the time is at hand. He that is unjust, let him be unjust still: and he which is filthy, let him be filthy still: and he that is righteous, let him be righteous still: and he that is holy, let him be holy still. And, behold, I come quickly; and my reward is with me, to give every man according as his work shall be. I am Alpha and Omega, the beginning and the end, the first and the last. Blessed are they that do his commandments, that they may have right to the tree of life, and may enter in through the gates into the city" (Revelation 21:1, 2, 27; 22:10–14).**

The Holy Spirit directed John to conclude God's revelation to man with a gracious yet sober reminder that entering God's eternal presence to dwell in the city He has prepared for the redeemed is conditional.

> **"For I testify unto every man that heareth the words of the prophecy of this book, If any man shall add unto these things, God shall add unto him the plagues that are written in this book: and if any man shall take away from the words of the book of this prophecy, God shall take away his part out of the book of life, and out of the holy city, and from the things which are written in this book" (Revelation 22:18, 19).**

We become God's sons and are "**translated . . . into the kingdom of his dear Son" (Colossians 1:13)** when, by God's marvelous grace, we are born again of His Spirit. But that does not place us outside of the probation under which all men on earth serve during their entire mature lifetime. During these years man continually exercises his will and shows or proves his commitment to God's will, or the lack of it. Revelation 22:18, 19 quoted above shows that the probation continues in force until death or the return of the Lord.

ANOTHER ETERNAL ABODE

There is yet another prepared place, an eternal abode. Jesus teaches us that it is **"prepared for the devil and his angels" (Matthew 25:41).** It likewise is prepared by God.

Jesus' teaching frequently pointed out the need to prepare by righteous living for the Judgment. In Matthew 25 this emphasis is especially marked. Jesus depicts a judgment scene when He comes with His angels.

> **"Then shall he sit upon the throne of his glory: and before him shall be gathered all nations: and he shall separate them one from another, as a shepherd divideth his sheep from the goats: and he shall set the sheep on his right hand, but the goats on the left. Then shall the King say unto them on his right hand, Come, ye blessed of my Father, inherit the kingdom prepared for you from the foundation of the world" (Matthew 25:31–34).**

The **sheep** did not understand when it was that they had served Him as He explained to them. Nor did the **goats** understand when it was that they had failed to serve Him.

> **"Then shall he say also unto them on the**

left hand, Depart from me, ye cursed, into everlasting fire, prepared for the devil and his angels. . . . Then shall they also answer him, saying, Lord, when saw we thee an hungred, or athirst, or a stranger, or naked, or sick, or in prison, and did not minister unto thee? Then shall he answer them, saying, Verily I say unto you, Inasmuch as ye did it not to one of the least of these, ye did it not to me. And these shall go away into everlasting punishment: but the righteous into life eternal" (Matthew 25:41, 44–46).

David also testifies of the eternal abode of the wicked.

"The Lord is known by the judgment which he executeth: the wicked is snared in the work of his own hands. . . . The wicked shall be turned into hell, and all the nations that forget God" (Psalm 9:16, 17).

Satan will finally be cast into this awful place. John describes the unending, eternal suffering there.

"And the devil that deceived them was cast into the lake of fire and brimstone, where the beast and the false prophet are, and shall be tormented day and night for ever and ever"

(Revelation 20:10).

The pain a human being suffers from exposure to fire is perhaps the most excruciating of all pain. Brimstone is sulfur. Trying to breathe in the presence of burning sulfur is very painful and stifling; it burns with a suffocating odor.

When God punished the people of Sodom and Gomorrah, He rained fire and brimstone upon them. That was of short duration. But the eternal punishment will be the suffering of fire and brimstone "**for ever and ever.**"

After the devil is cast into the lake of fire, the great white throne judgment of all men shall take place. John writes:

> **"And I saw a great white throne, and him that sat on it, from whose face the earth and the heaven fled away; and there was found no place for them. And I saw the dead, small and great, stand before God; and the books were opened: and another book was opened, which is the book of life: and the dead were judged out of those things which were written in the books, according to their works. And the sea gave up the dead which were in it; and death and hell delivered up the dead which were in**

them: and they were judged every man according to their works. And death and hell were cast into the lake of fire. This is the second death. And whosoever was not found written in the book of life was cast into the lake of fire" (Revelation 20:11–15).

My dear Reader, prepare now for the prepared place for those who are redeemed through the precious blood of Christ and live by the power of His resurrection. Satan cannot stand before the redeemed, because **"greater is he that is in** [them]**, than he that is in the world" (1 John 4:4).** When Jesus Christ abides within the heart of a person, He rules and reigns there in righteousness. He alone can keep us from serving sin, the flesh, the world, and Satan. Jesus wants to do that for you, that when He comes for His own, He may take you too as a part of His prepared bride.

18.

"Be Ye Also Ready"

A final appeal should be made to basic honesty.

"Behold, thou desirest truth in the inward parts" (Psalm 51:6).

Jesus, in the parable of the sower, indicated that whether a person brings forth fruit depends on the response to truth in the heart. This helps us to understand why people are where they are in relation to His Word. Whether the seed will grow and bring forth fruit depends on how the soil is tended. Of the fourth soil type, Jesus said:

"But that on the good ground are they, which in an *honest and good heart,* having heard the word, keep it, and bring forth fruit with patience" (Luke 8:15).

We have looked at many Scriptures to see what God says. Now God expects from us a response that shows that we believe what He says, and that we do not lean to our own understanding.

Do we want to face God, and take a chance? Suppose God does expect of us what these Scriptures say. And suppose we have not taken Him seriously. How terrible that would be! For years we would have known these truths, and, as the rich man in hell (Luke 16:27, 28), we would recall that in our pride we had decided that God surely does not mean what He says. We would then remember such Scriptures as:

"The wicked shall be turned into hell, and all the nations that forget God" (Psalm 9:17).

"The Lord shall endure for ever: he hath prepared his throne for judgment. And he shall judge the world in righteousness" (Psalm 9:7, 8).

Will we risk our "interpretation," or will we believe and act on what God actually, literally says? Which is the safe course?

ARE YOU RESPONDING TO GOD AND HIS WORD WITH ALL HONESTY IN YOUR HEART?

Consider a few searching questions:

Have you forsaken all for Christ?

Or are you holding to some small or cheap item and thus forfeiting your right to the gift of eternal life?

Are you trying to impose yourself and your own lifestyle on the holiness of God?

Are you trying to make some cheap god of our great Almighty God, the Creator of the heavens and the earth?

Are you facing God's message of salvation with "**an honest and good heart**"?

Or, are you deciding what seems reasonable to your own mind and expecting God to accept your terms?

Absolute honesty with God will bring security and rest within. With it will come reproaches, hardships, inconveniences, and persecution—all of which Jesus Christ bore for you.

> **"Yea, and all that will live godly in Christ Jesus shall suffer persecution" (2 Timothy 3:12).**

"And if the righteous scarcely be saved, where shall the ungodly and the sinner appear?" **(1 Peter 4:18)**

"Therefore be ye also ready: for in such an hour as ye think not the Son of man cometh" (Matthew 24:44).